Chilli Notes

To my parents, without whom I'd be toast;
To Tati and Twiglet with love.

Thomasina Miers

Chilli Notes

**Recipes to warm the heart
(not burn the tongue)**

HODDER &
STOUGHTON

First published in Great Britain in 2014 by Hodder & Stoughton
An Hachette UK company

1

Text Copyright © Thomasina Miers 2014
Photography Copyright © Tara Fisher 2014

A CIP catalogue record for this title is available from the British Library

Hardback ISBN 978 1 444 77688 1
Ebook ISBN 978 1 444 77689 8

Editorial Director Nicky Ross
Project Editor Sarah Hammond
Copy Editor Zelda Turner
Design & Art Direction BuroCreative
Photographer Tara Fisher
Food Stylist Emma Miller
Props Stylist Tabitha Hawkins

Typeset in Cheltenham by Bitstream and Cheltenham by ITC

Printed and bound in China by C&C Offset Printing Co., Ltd.

Hodder & Stoughton policy is to use papers that are natural, renewable and
recyclable products and made from wood grown in sustainable forests.
The logging and manufacturing processes are expected to conform to the
environmental regulations of the country of origin.

Hodder & Stoughton Ltd
338 Euston Road
London NW1 3BH

www.hodder.co.uk

Contents

Flavour and Heat: a story of addiction   6

The Chilli Hot List *(And What to Use if You Can't Find Them)*   14

Cooking with Chillies   18

Store Cupboard Essentials   20

1. Starters and Nibbles   22

2. Quick Fixes   42

3. Soups and Other One Pots   60

4. From the Store Cupboard   78

5. Cooking for Friends   100

6. Weekend Treats   122

7. Comfort Eating   142

8. Standby Sauces, Salsas (and Sprinkles)   160

9. Perfect Foils   180

10. Puddings and A Few Drinks   192

Stockists   220

Index   221

Acknowledgements   224

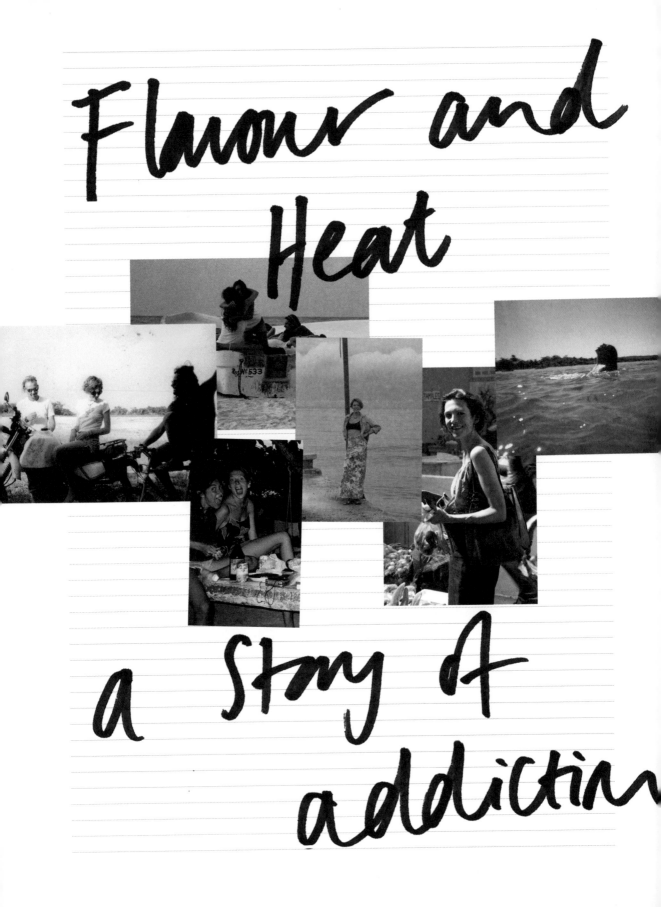

Flour and Heat

a story of addiction

I can trace my love affair with the chilli pepper back to my late teens when I made my first trip outside of Europe, a trip casually undertaken with a girlfriend from school that, unbeknownst to me, would shape my entire adult life. In those days I was wild; I wanted to suck the essence out of life, to dance all night, drink cocktails galore and always have the most fun. I wanted to do, not be, to participate, not watch; I never wanted to be on the sidelines.

This raison d'être seemed to have shaped my early love affair with cooking; I couldn't see the point of playing in the nursery and later on in the school playground. In the kitchen, on the other hand, I had a purpose: cooking I could understand, it was an affirmative action. My passion for food and cooking led to my love for travelling and exploring other cuisines and so to my early interest in and attachment to chillies, for, unwittingly, on that first properly long trip away from home I had arrived at the chilli capital of the world: Mexico.

Whilst wimpish fellow travellers might avoid the local streetfood and, perish the thought, the fresh ceviches and salads, I would consciously and precociously eat every type of taco and edible insect I could find. The more local and regional the food, the more I wanted to try it; the more hardcore the ingredient, the more I wanted to love it. If I drank the nights away I ate the days away too, partly to soak up the excesses of the nights before, but mainly because I just couldn't get enough of the food; particularly the chillies.

I discovered that chilli-spiked ceviche marinated in copious quantities of fresh citrus juice was a miracle cure-all; that hot salsa on warm tortilla chips was the ultimate pick-me-up; that richly spiced and headily chillied sauces on slow-cooked meats seemed to reach out and comfort me to my very core when I was feeling most homesick. Wherever we stayed I would spend a large chunk of my time investigating the best places to eat. When by the sea I would seek out the stall that had the freshest-looking fish and I would liberally pour over the hottest of the cantina's table sauces that I could find. In cities and towns I would track down the busiest taco stands with the best salsas.

My heat tolerance was like a badge of honour; I was as macho about chilli heat as I am now passionate about chilli flavour. I would challenge everyone around me to chilli-eating competitions and take pride in being able to out-hot the feistiest boys. The red-hot chilli pepper provided natural highs that I became hooked on.

Living in Mexico and then when I went on to open Wahaca, I started to learn about the nuances of flavour, and the different varieties of chillies that are being grown across the UK. Now I revel in their versatility, both as a cook and as someone who loves to eat. A light smattering of fresh chilli can delicately pep up a pile of silky cumin-and-cinnamon-spiced aubergine; dark, tobacco-flavoured chillies can add deep, mysterious tones to molten chocolate; smoky chillies can add body to slow-cooked, unctuous stews; sweet paprika adds earthiness to eggs, grilled flatbreads and sautéed greens.

Fresh chillies add excitement to the simplest ingredients and, in turn, the most frugal ingredients can coax out different aspects of a chilli's character: lime juice can add brightness and zest to fresh chillies; throw in some fresh peas and broad beans and you get sweetness and innocence; soy and sesame make chillies darker and more intense. Fresh mint and parsley, or a scattering of fresh coriander lends them an exotic Middle Eastern, Mexican or Indian flavour.

A natural high

Chillies also pack in the nutrients. Quite apart from the hair of the dog, a Bloody Mary tastes so good on a Sunday morning because it is bursting with vitamins A and C, with iron, potassium and magnesium, and with anti-oxidants, making it the perfect tonic if you're feeling tired and overdone. Studies have shown that chillies lower cholesterol, that they possess anti-carcinogenic, anti-bacterial, analgesic and anti-diabetic properties. To discover that chillies might be the next superfood is only to confirm a hunch I have long held.

It is the neurotoxin capsaicin – the substance that makes a chilli hot – that is largely responsible for the fruit's amazing medicinal properties. In 1912, the American chemist Wilbur Scoville developed the first system for measuring the strength of chillies. His scale is designed around the number of times a chilli extract needs diluting before it no longer burns your mouth. A sweet red pepper, which contains no capsaicin, scores 0 Scovilles, a jalapeño pepper is 2,500 to 4,000 and a Mexican habanero is anywhere between 200,000 and 500,000. The more capsaicin the hotter the pepper and the higher the anti-oxidant levels.

When we eat capsaicin it hits the pain receptors on the tongue's nerve cells, which sends a message to the brain – it is essentially a chemical attack on our nerves. In response, our body releases endorphins and analgesics to cope with the pain, creating that natural high that chilli-fiends love. Some people can't stand chillies and a minority are even allergic to them. But with constant eating, a chilli-lover's nerve cells will become gradually desensitised to the pain so that you need increasing amounts of chilli to provide that natural high. Once you get used to the heat on your tongue the sensation becomes pleasant and that is why in ancient Aztec and Mayan societies, chillies were considered to be aphrodisiacs, producing an unmistakable feel-good rush – endorphins are not known as the 'pleasure hormone' for nothing. Even my two-year-old has started on the slippery slope and complains noisily if we don't share our Bloody Marys – only the Virgin version for her!

Chillies have other health benefits too: it seems capsaicin naturally curbs the appetite (whilst you are eating chillies at least). My completely unscientific theory is that by intensifying the flavour and punch of food you need far less of it to feel satisfied. Chillies are also supposed to stimulate the metabolism and the warming effect they have on the body mean that it burns calories faster. So not only are chillies packed with vitamins and minerals but – like green tea and caffeine – eaten in the right quantities they can help you keep a trim figure.

World domination

Chillies largely originated in Mexico, although some varieties can be traced back to parts of Central and South America too, as early as 5000 BC. A member of the nightshade family of flowering plants, along with the potato, the tomato and the aubergine, it is thought that chillies evolved to make capsaicin to deter fungus growth on the fruit (which is why chilli sauces last so long in the cupboard). But the capsaicin found in the chilli's placenta – the pale white membrane that grows along the veins leading from the stalk, that holds the seeds – also serves to deter mammals from eating the fruit. When mammals eat chillies the seeds are chewed up or broken down in their guts and destroyed. Wild birds, on the other hand, swallow the seeds whole and scatter them far and wide in their droppings, ensuring that the plants travel and prosper. Birds can happily eat the hottest chillies, as they are immune to the irritating effects of capsaicin.

Of course the story of why two billion people are eating chillies around the world is a little more toothy than that. The spread of chilli peppers provides a telling map of the first waves of globalisation in the fifteenth and sixteenth centuries, when the Portuguese and Spanish were the major world players. The two superpowers would sponsor merchants to travel far and wide to expand their empires and establish control of trade with the Orient.

The tale starts when Christopher Columbus was looking for a new trade route to India, on behalf of the Spanish crown. Stumbling across the Americas instead, he brought the chilli back to Spain, confusing it with a spice and calling it 'pimiento' (Spanish for 'pepper'), after the highly valuable pepper plant he had hoped to find in India. Ultimately though it was the Portuguese who were responsible for the chilli's spread across the globe. At the time, Portugal was the dominant maritime power – the Portuguese merchant Bartomoleu Dias was the first man to sail around the southernmost tip of Africa, and fellow explorer Vasco da Gama became the first European to establish the long-awaited sea route to India. By the 1500s, the Portuguese were regularly exporting chilli

peppers from Brazil, stopping in various African ports along the way.

India, with a similar climate to Mexico and Brazil, took to the chilli plant with alacrity; so much so that it wasn't until the nineteenth century that the British discovered that chillies originated in Mexico, not India. The Portuguese were also busy colonising parts of Africa, which provided crucial landing stages en route to India and further East. The Africans already had a highly popular spice called 'grains of paradise' which was citrusy and peppery; the move to chillies was smooth. As the Portuguese slave trade grew, and local populations were shipped across the world, chilli plants would accompany them. The chilli had begun its inexorable path to world domination.

In London's two big wholesale markets, New Covent Garden and Spitalfields, you can see these global influences even today. These markets supply the hundreds of grocers and local markets that make up London's thriving food scene and also the restaurants that cater to our hugely diverse, multicultural population. Visiting these markets is like being teleported into a different country for a few hours. Boxes stamped with labels and logos from all over the world pile up as far as the eye can see. They are filled with exotic fruits like mangoes and pineapple, and with extraordinary, unfamiliar vegetables and chillies of all different shapes and sizes. These crates are destined for the East End to feed Bangladeshi and Turkish communities; for West London to feed Japanese, African and Indian communities; and for Central London for Chinese, Malaysian and Thai restaurants.

As Britons get more adventurous with food, as we travel and assimilate cultures and learn from ethnic communities around the UK, we are discovering ever more about global cuisine. The street food revolution that is hitting Britain right now feeds this curiosity and offers us food from the United States, Thailand, China, Mexico, India and beyond.

This book is not an encyclopedia of chillies. Mexico alone has over 200 varieties and so great is the chilli craze that is currently sweeping the world that new varieties are being bred all the time. In this book I have instead tried to use an edited number of chillies to give you an insight into how they can season and flavour the simplest of everyday ingredients. I hope you will find that it is full of recipes that excite and tantalise, comfort and warm, and will win over even those who profess to loathe chilli heat. Forget about crazy hot sauces that knock you for six, think of this book as a companion to transform weekday nights with food that is just a little bit more exciting than usual. Think of the chilli as your exotic bedfellow to add wonderful, unusual notes to your home-cooked food. Feed the family with these simple recipes, but feed them with panache.

Chillies and children

Many of these recipes can be toned up or down according to your family's particular tolerance to heat – as with all things taste is incredibly personal – but please don't think that you can't cook these recipes for your children just because they have a touch of heat. My fourteen-year-old nephew hated chillies for years but with enough of my cooking he slowly came round and is now an avid fan. My daughter Tati's favourite drink is the Virgin Mary. It is amazing what children can develop a taste for when given the chance.

A note on heat

You may notice that the recipes in this book have different colour titles. This is a rough heat scale, so the more yellow the mellower the recipe, and the redder it is the hotter it is! You can scale the heat up and down to suit your own tastebuds.

Cayenne pepper

Bird's eye chillies

PIMENTÓN DE LA VERA
DENOMINACIÓN DE ORIGEN PROTEGIDA
LA DALIA
1913
2013
Picante - Hot - Piquant
Peso neto · Net Weight · Poid Net
70 grs / 2.469 oz

pimentón
(picante)

Pasilla

Jalapeño

Sichuan
chillies

Sichuan pepper

Chipotle

Fresh chillies
(mixed)

Chile de árbol

Kashmiri
chillies

Turkish Chilli Flakes
(Aleppo)

Pimentón de la Vera
Denomination of Origin Protected
SANTO DOMINGO

Quality
SWEET

pimentón
(dulce)

Habanero

Ancho

The Chilli Hot List

(And What to Use if You Can't Find Them)

Here is the list of chillies that I've used in this book. When an ingredients list says 'fresh red chilli' you can use the generic ones you find in the supermarket, using more or less depending on how much heat you like. Some grocers and supermarkets stock little jars of ready-chopped chillies as a cheat's ingredient which are fine too, but I would say try to use fresh when I suggest fresh and dried when I use dried. In general, fresh are better at adding a sparkle of heat on top of food, in particular salads and fresh salsas, whilst dried chillies add a lovely background heat; I like to use them in slower cooked recipes and in the bases of soups and stews. If I've mentioned a specific chilli (for example, chile de árbol) it's because I think this has the right flavour/depth for that recipe, but please don't be put off from cooking the dish if you don't have it. Have a look at the substitution guide at the end of each entry and, if in doubt, add any type of chilli you have at home; you can gradually start learning about the particular ones you like. Taste, after all, is a personal thing. As with all recipes, removing the seeds will allow you to appreciate the flavour of the chilli without being exposed to quite so much of its heat.

Ancho (dried)

Heat (out of 10): 4

Poblano chillies are large fresh chillies, similar in appearance to green peppers but a much darker green and with a thinner skin. When dried, a poblano is transformed into the **ancho** chilli, a round, dark red chilli with fruity tones. Rich in flavour and fairly mild in heat (although they are steadily getting hotter), an ancho adds sweetness and depth of flavour to marinades, salsas and moles.

What to use instead: Spanish dried red peppers like the ñora or the guindilla have a similar flavour to the ancho, being both sweet and not too hot.

Bird's eye chillies (fresh)

Heat: 9

Bird's eye chillies are used extensively in Thai, Lao, Khmer and Vietnamese cooking and also in parts of India (particularly in Kerala). They are small but with a ferocious heat to them. They also have a subtly fruity taste. Thanks to the UK's ethnic makeup these chillies are widely available here and, unlike the more generic, unlabelled chillies often sold in supermarkets with hugely varying heat levels, bird's eye chillies are reliably fiery, so you know what you are playing with.

What to use instead: Any fresh chilli will do, although you will have to use plenty of regular fresh chillies to get the same heat levels as a few bird's eye. A habanero/Scotch bonnet is even hotter than a bird's eye but it has quite a strong citrusy flavour that can be overpowering, so tread carefully. You can also use the long green chillies you find in Asian grocers, whose heat lies somewhere between a Scotch bonnet and a standard red chilli; these are much bigger, so use a third for each bird's eye.

Cayenne pepper (dried)

Heat: 9

Cayenne pepper is arguably from the most famous chilli of all, the cayenne, dried and ground. Whilst it is hot it is not blisteringly so: a little can be sprinkled onto dishes to add a light sparkle of heat. I particularly like to use cayenne in puddings where I don't want to confuse the palate with too many different flavours. It is a much better bet than a generic chilli powder, which can be a blend of chillies and spices and tends to overwhelm the flavour of the food you add it to.

What to use instead: Any type of chilli powder.

Chile de árbol (dried)

Heat: 9

I use **chile de árbol** (named after the tree-like bush it grows from) like other people use black pepper. It has a wonderfully versatile dry, fiery heat that adds a touch of peppery seasoning to stocks, stews and sauces. Whilst chiles de árbol are hot, using one in a large soup or stew will add only a gentle peppery heat through the dish; if you wanted a really hot dish you might add two. When chiles de árbol are toasted more of their flavour comes out and they become wonderfully nutty; they are a failsafe variety to use for making chilli oil and hot chilli sauces (see page 176). You see this chilli cropping up all over restaurant menus in California, where influences from Mexico (and Korea) merge with the modern, seasonal approach to food first espoused by Alice Waters thirty years ago.

What to use instead: Try using two to three pepperoncini, the tiny Italian dried chillies, for every chile de árbol, or use half a teaspoon of dried chilli flakes or cayenne pepper instead.

Chipotle (dried)

Heat: 8

The **chipotle**, or smoked, dried jalapeño, is probably one of Mexico's best-known chillies (its name stems from the words 'chilli' and 'smoke' in the native Indian language Nahuatl). Although there are several different varieties of chipotle, the one that I use is known as the mora. It has an intoxicating fiery flavour that is delicious in salsas and mayonnaises and makes the incredible chipotles en adobo (see page 169) that can quickly become an indispensable ingredient in your cupboard.

What to use instead: Dry roast a couple of bird's eye chillies with a plum tomato in a hot frying pan. Whizz them up with a teaspoon of sweet smoked paprika and a good pinch of salt.

Dried chilli flakes

Heat: 7 or 8

Dried chilli flakes can be made from pretty much any type of dried red chilli – it is almost impossible to tell what type you are getting, and I have never seen them labelled in shops. They have a great advantage over chilli powder in that they seem to keep for longer, perhaps because they are not so finely ground. They tend to be hot. They are a great standby to have in the larder and make a great substitute for chile de árbol. I would say a generous half teaspoon of chilli flakes is the equivalent to one chile de árbol (with seeds in).

What to use instead: Korean gochugaru chilli flakes are similarly mild and flavourful. If not de-seed and roast a chile de árbol or a couple of pepperoncino and crumble for a hotter result.

Fresh red chillies

Heat: various

Supermarkets stock generic **fresh red chillies** and their levels of heat vary wildly. They are great for adding a fresh burst of spice to food but you do need to check how hot individual chillies are (see page 18) before working out how much to use. As with all chillies, you can always add more if your food is not quite hot enough.

What to use instead: Any fresh chilli will do. Asian grocers stock fresh long red chillies, which are the equivalent to two supermarket chillies, and long green chillies, which are much hotter than bog standard fresh chillies.

Habanero / Scotch bonnet (fresh)

Heat: 10

Habaneros are from the Yucatan and are the first Mexican chilli to win Protected Denomination of Origin status. They are almost identical in appearance and flavour to the **Scotch bonnet** and look like brightly coloured Chinese lanterns, in orange, red and yellow. Whilst they are pretty to look at they are devilishly hot with a wonderful citrusy note to them that is accentuated with roasting. Eat judiciously.

What to use instead: Bird's eye chillies have similar heat levels, or use whatever fresh chilli you can find, keeping the seeds in, and add as much heat as you like with cayenne pepper or dried chilli flakes.

Jalapeño (fresh)

Heat: 8

Green, curvy, fresh and spicy, these fiery chillies can pack quite a punch, although the heat won't last long (and can vary hugely from one chilli to another). **Jalapeños** are increasingly available in supermarkets and are hotter than the unnamed fresh chillies of a similar size that you see sold next to them.

What to use instead: Substitute with any fresh green chilli or a bird's eye chilli.

Kashmiri chillies (dried)

Heat: 4

In India the aromatic **Kashmiri chilli** is famous for its delicious, aromatic flavour (a little like paprika) and the deep vibrant colour it gives to dishes like the Kashmiri classic, Rogan Josh, a recipe with roots in Persia. The chilli is milder than the other Indian favourite, cayenne, and is therefore incredibly versatile and used throughout India and other parts of South East Asia. Kashmiri chillies are ground or puréed and then added to recipes. They can be found in Asian supermarkets or online.

What to use instead: Kashmiri chillies can be substituted with Korean or Sichuan chillies, or mix half a chile de árbol and one guajillo chilli for each Kashmiri chilli.

Pasilla (dried)

Heat: 6

Pasilla chillies have a herbaceous, raisin-like taste with undertones of tobacco that adds huge complexity to food. In Mexico they are part of the chilli trio used to make moles (with the ancho and the guajillo) but they are also wonderful on their own thanks to their unique flavour. Try them out in my dark, squidgy chocolate brownies (page 214) or the shin of beef on page 140. You will be bowled over by their flavour.

What to use instead: Whilst there are no substitutes for the pasilla taste you can replicate their heat by using a teaspoon of Turkish chilli flakes or half a teaspoon of regular chilli flakes for every two teaspoons of pasilla flakes. An equal quantity of ancho chilli will give food a similar body to the pasillas but you will need to add a pinch of chilli flakes or cayenne pepper to get a similar heat.

Sichuan pepper and Sichuan chillies (dried)

Heat: 5

Sichuan pepper was used in China long before the black pepper that we are familiar with. It comes from the dried berries of a shrub that grows in mountainous areas and has a woody citrusy flavour and a tingling effect on the tongue that is far more vivid when the berries are fresh. If you can get the fresh peppercorns online (see page 220), store them in the freezer and freshly grind your own pepper (the powder loses its fragrance very quickly, even when stored somewhere dry and airtight). **Sichuan chillies**, which are fairly mild in heat, have a deep, rounded flavour that complements the citrusy notes of Sichuan pepper. They are often used together with garlic and ginger in Sichuan cooking and are highly prized for their colour, which stains food a deep terracotta red.

What to use instead: Thanks to Sichuan cookery expert Fuchsia Dunlop, I discovered that the tongue-numbing, mouth-smarting combination of Sichuan pepper and (the hard-to-find) dried Sichuan chilli can be recreated at home with the help of my old friend, the Mexican chile de árbol. For recipes that feature Sichuan pepper on its own, there is no real substitute, but Sichuan pepper is easy to get hold of these days, either online or in larger supermarkets and delis.

Spanish smoked paprika (pimentón)

Heat: 6 and 2

Spanish paprika has a big advantage over other European paprikas because it is usually dried by smoking it over wood, which gives it a distinctive smoky character. It therefore makes a great substitute for chipotles when you are looking to add a brooding touch of smoke to your food as well as that chilli kick. The paprika normally comes in two versions, pimentón picante – a hot version (about 6/10 on the heatscale) and pimentón dulce – a sweet version (about 2/10). Picante is hot enough to give your tongue a gentle workout whilst the dulce is soft and sweet-natured and adds a wonderfully mellow, smoky edge to whatever it touches.

What to use instead: Normal paprika can be used in place of hot smoked paprika, but you will lose the smoky taste. Chipotles provide the same smoky character as smoked paprika but are pretty hot so only use in place of pimentón picante.

Turkish chilli flakes (kirmizi biber) (dried)

Heat: 4

I discovered **Turkish chilli flakes** on my first trip to Istanbul a few years ago. 'Kirmizi biber' means red pepper and the flakes come from dried red chillies that are usually mild in taste. The two predominant types used are 'urfa', a deep crimson, almost black chilli that is sweet and smoky in taste and the 'Aleppo chilli', named after the city of Aleppo in Syria, which is a light burgundy colour and has a subtly sweet, mild flavour. The chillies are de-seeded, salted and semi-dried before being crushed and rubbed with oil. They are ubiquitous in Turkish and Syrian cooking, sprinkled over meat dishes or over yoghurt and labnehs to serve as an accompaniment to food. Sometimes the flakes are toasted in the frying pan to accentuate the chilli's flavour and heat.

What to use instead: Any dried chilli flake, a chile de árbol or a couple of pepperoncino chillies. Dry roast them first to match the depth of flavour that Turkish chillies have.

Cooking with Chillies

Finely chopped or diced fresh chillies can be scattered like spicy stardust over food. Dry roasted, they give a robust, charred edge (and sweet core) to table salsas. Dried chillies can be ground into a powder to add heat and vibrancy to food. Or they can be toasted to bring out their flavour, and soaked in boiling water to rehydrate them before being added to loose, wet pastes for soups, stews and sauces, or blitzed with vinegar and herbs to make some seriously kick-ass salsas. Here's all you need to know to get started:

How to test chillies for heat

It is often wise to check the power of chillies before you get too carried away with them – even within one variety the heat level can vary enormously. To be sure of what you are getting, slice off the tip of the chilli and have a taste. The end has the least heat so a nibble of this and you will get an idea of how hot the rest of the chilli is. If you want to tone down the heat but keep the flavour, remove the seeds and membrane of the chilli and only use the flesh.

How to rehydrate dry chillies

All dried chillies taste best when they are toasted before being rehydrated, just as you would toast whole spices before you grind them.

1 First, tear open the chillies and remove their stems and seeds (in certain chilli sauces you can toast and grind chilli seeds to add a deep, chilli heat and flavour, so do keep them if you like to experiment).

2 Tear the chillies into a few, smaller pieces that can lie flat in a pan. Heat a heavy-bottomed frying pan over a medium heat; if it becomes too hot the chillies will burn and become bitter tasting. Add the chillies, in batches if you are using lots, and toast them for about a minute on both sides, until they puff up a little, darken in colour and start smelling fragrant. If you over-toast them they will burn and make the dish you put them in taste bitter.

3 Once they are gently toasted, cover the chillies with boiling water and let them soak for about 15 minutes until soft. Drain them, discarding the soaking water, and purée as per the recipe instructions.

Note: chipotle chillies are tougher than most dried chillies and need to be simmered in water for 25–30 minutes to completely soften before puréeing.

How to finely dice or slice fresh chillies

To dice fresh chillies, chop the stem off the chilli, then cut the fruit in half lengthways. With a small, sharp knife, cut out the membrane at the top of the chilli and remove it, along with the seeds. Cut each chilli half into long, skinny ribbons and then cut the ribbons across into tiny dice.

To finely slice, chop the stem off the chilli, then slice the fruit into thin rounds. Run a chopping knife across the slices several times until you get rough pieces. To finely chop, keep chopping until they become very small pieces!

How to wash your hands after handling chillies

If you've been handling lots of really hot chillies you will find that the capsaicin seems to penetrate the fingertips and is difficult to budge even with vigorous scrubbing in soap and water. At this stage (and before you go to the loo or rub your eyes) rub some fine salt and olive oil into your fingers for a few minutes and then wash with soap and water.

Toast them for about a minute on all
sides, until they puff up, darken in
colour and start smelling fragrant

Store Cupboard Essentials

Black pepper

Pepper is often overlooked as a spice as it is used so much but it is worth seeking out good-quality peppercorns and always grinding them fresh over food. Its flavour is wonderful and I use it rather like I use chillies, to lightly pep up the flavour of food.

Flaky sea salt

There is always plenty of controversy surrounding salt but if you are eating a diet that is high in fresh ingredients and low in processed foods your diet will be naturally lower in salt. I therefore salt food liberally; it improves the taste of both sweet and savoury food and whilst it is not apparent that a flaky sea salt is any better for you, it is much easier to use in moderation than a processed fine grain salt and has a much more enticing, scrunchy texture.

Eggs

I use medium free-range eggs in these recipes, unless otherwise noted.

Fat

Fat in moderation is essential to our survival and some fats, like nut, rapeseed and olive oils, provide the body with essential nutrients. Fat makes food taste better by carrying flavour for longer and giving a moist texture to food when we eat it. This is why cooks dress food with oil just before serving, whether it is extra virgin olive oil, salad dressings, flavoured butter or tempered, spiced oil. I tend to use olive oil, vegetable oil, sesame oil and butter when cooking. I never use spreads or margarines, which are artificial in both flavour and make up.

Extra virgin olive oil

Extra virgin olive oil loses its flavour when overheated but when gently warmed or used cold, it has a wonderful grassy flavour that improves the taste of food immeasurably. Invest in a good bottle of extra virgin olive oil, avoiding supermarket own brands, and use it strictly for dressing food not for cooking. A little goes a long way so it won't end up breaking the bank.

Tamarind

Tamarind is the sticky, pulpy fruit from a tree native to tropical parts of Africa and is widely used in Indian, South East Asian and Mexican cooking. Its flavour is refreshingly sour, like lime, with a sweetness to it that adds a great dimension to food. It is sold either in blocks of the raw pulp that needs to be rehydrated and made into a fresh purée, or in jars of concentrated paste. The fresh purée always tastes better.

Anchovies

Anchovies are small fish that add tremendous depth of flavour to food. Stocks of anchovies are now in decline so look for jars decorated with the MSC logo and buy them packed in oil.

Kalamata olives

Kalamata are a particular variety of black olive that have an amazingly rich and oily flavour. Buy them whole, with their stones in; olives that are stoned and stored in brine typically have very little flavour and are not worth your hard-earned pennies.

Tahini

The ground paste of sesame seeds is both delicious and extremely nutritious and is particularly high in calcium. It has a nutty, rich flavour and jars of it last for months in the fridge.

Pomegranate molasses

The concentrated juices of fresh pomegranates add a delightfully sweet, sticky and slightly sour flavour to dishes. The beautiful fruit are mentioned in many ancient texts and grow on small trees that originate in Iran but are now grown all over the world. Homemade molasses are both delicious and very easy to make but bottles of readymade molasses are also widely available.

Make your own pomegranate molasses
Whizz the seeds of 3 pomegranates in a blender and pour through a sieve. You should get about 350ml of juice but the amount will vary according to the size of the fruit. For every 250ml of juice add 1 tbsp lemon juice and 2 tbsp caster sugar. Bring to the boil in a saucepan and simmer briskly until the mixture has reduced to a wonderful, syrupy consistency. Cool and store in the refrigerator.

Parmesan

Parmigiano-Reggiano is a hard, granular cheese made in particular provinces of Italy. It adds huge depth of flavour to food so it is worth always having a small block of it in the fridge, well wrapped in cheese cloth or greaseproof paper. If you can't stretch to Parmesan, Gran Padano makes an acceptable substitute.

Soy Sauce

A sauce made from fermented soy beans and roast grains, soy sauce gives food a deliciously salty, rich, meaty flavour. Light soy sauce is ideal for seasoning food and for use in dipping sauces whilst dark soy sauce has been aged for longer, is less salty and more sweet so it is good for braising meats (its flavour also develops with cooking).

Miso Paste

A traditional Japanese seasoning made from fermented soy beans and rice. It is most readily available as a paste and comes in several different forms. My favourite is a sweet version made from brown rice; it is full-bodied, full of umami taste and adds tremendous depth of flavour to food.

Sichuan chilli bean paste

Made from salt-fermented chillies and broad beans, this paste is one of the essential ingredients in Sichuanese cooking. Lee Kum Kee makes a light version but if you are near a Chinese supermarket it is worth trying to seek out a Sichuanese version.

Chilli oil

Chilli oil is used throughout Sichuanese and Mexican cookery. You can make your own in very little time (see page 163) and it keeps indefinitely, but it is also widely available in specialist shops. In Mexico, chile de árbol chillies are used to make a particularly spicy version whilst in Sichuan a milder oil is used as a relish for noodles, dumplings and cold dishes, made with Sichuan or Korean chillies.

Thai red curry paste

Thai red curry paste is a standard paste used to season Thai curries. Its main ingredients are garlic, shallots, red chillies, galangal, shrimp paste, kaffir lime and spices. Good grocers and supermarkets now stock really good Thai curry pastes in the chilled sections and it keeps well in both the fridge and freezer.

Fish Sauce

Fish sauce is made from salting and fermenting anchovies and other small fish. It adds extraordinary depth of flavour to food and is used much as we use salt in South East Asian cookery. Buy brands that are a light, amber colour – if the liquid has become too dark it will taste overly fishy.

1

Starters and nibbles

Sometimes you want to start a meal with food that is easy and straightforward, so that you can relax and spend more time chatting than cooking. Then again, sometimes you fancy pulling out all the stops and spoiling your friends with food that you have really thought about and even splashed out on. Hopefully this chapter will satisfy both these impulses with simple, seasonal starters that are big and bold on flavour.

Perhaps the salt and pepper squid will grab your attention: a starter that takes minutes to cook but really packs a punch with a devilish Sichuan pepper and chilli hit. Surprise your guests with the sweet, wonderfully balanced black pudding and caramelised pear salad, with its smoky touch of paprika and subtle flavour. Go simple with the braised fennel and mascarpone bruschetta, or spectacular with the Caramelised scallop, avocado and orange salad; introduce a taste of India with the sautéed chickpea and mango salad or some Asian flavour with the Thai crab salad with Nam Jim dressing.

With a touch of intriguing spice, it's easy to start dinner with something light, appetising and delicious, perfect for getting the night off to an exotic start.

This is the perfect summer starter when peaches are ripe and juicy and you are short of time. It was inspired by a week I once spent at Finca Buenvino, a wonderful cooking school in southern Spain where the legendary Ibérico pigs are reared on a diet of acorns grown on the gnarly trees that decorate its rolling landscape. Made with this ham, Serrano, or Parma, it's great for lunch or supper, or as part of an al fresco mezze for friends.

Peach, cured ham and mozzarella bruschetta

Feeds 6

2 balls of buffalo mozzarella (about 250g)
4–5 tbsp extra virgin olive oil
30g Parmesan cheese, freshly grated
1 fresh red chilli, de-seeded and finely chopped
A handful of mint leaves, roughly chopped
6 slices of sourdough or dense country loaf
1 garlic clove, halved
3 ripe peaches, halved and de-stoned
150g Ibérico, Serrano or Parma ham slices

Tear apart the mozzarella and mix it with 3 tablespoons of the olive oil, the Parmesan, the chilli and a good sprinkling of salt and freshly ground black pepper. Mix the mint with the mozzarella. Cut each peach half into 3 wedges.

Toast the bread on a chargrill or in a toaster and rub the cut side of the garlic all over it. Drizzle with some extra virgin olive oil then top with the mozzarella salad, peach wedges and ham. Serve at once.

Sweet, slow-braised fennel with its caramelised, white wine juices; salty, fatty Parmesan cheese; the slight spice of smoked paprika and the sweetness of currants; this is a dead easy but utterly delicious topping for bruschetta. Your friends will think it the height of sophistication and you will giggle to yourself at how easy it was.

Braised fennel and mascarpone bruschetta with smoked paprika

Feeds 6 as a starter or 4 as a light lunch

6 medium fennel bulbs
16 Kalamata or other black olives, de-stoned
  and roughly chopped
200ml white wine
40g currants
6 sprigs of fresh oregano
1½ tsp hot smoked paprika
6 tbsp olive oil
200g mascarpone
50g Parmesan cheese or pecorino,
  freshly grated
4–6 slices of sourdough or dense country loaf
1 garlic clove, unpeeled and halved
Extra virgin olive oil
A handful of mint leaves, roughly chopped

Preheat the oven to 180°C/350°F/gas 4.

Trim each fennel bulb and cut into 6–8 pieces: you don't want enormous chunks as they will be harder to eat. Put the olives in a roasting pan with the fennel, white wine, currants, oregano and paprika. Season with salt and pepper and splash with the olive oil.

Cover the pan lightly with foil and roast in the oven for 30–35 minutes. Remove the foil and return to the oven for a further 10 minutes, until the fennel is golden.

Meanwhile, whip up the mascarpone with a fork and mix together with the Parmesan (or pecorino). When you are ready to eat, toast the bread on a chargrill or in a toaster and rub the cut side of the garlic all over it.
Drizzle with some extra virgin olive oil then smear each slice with a good dollop of the cheese mix. Top with the roasted fennel and the fresh mint.

Frying chickpeas brings out their nuttiness, and their naughtiness, for they are an otherwise virtuous pulse. This is my homage to the glorious tastes of India, mixing sweet mango and cherry tomato, fresh mint and cucumber with bursts of intense heat from the homemade blend of garam masala and finely chopped fresh chilli. I find this dish deeply satisfying but also light and summery: for me it's the perfect lunch.

Chickpea and mango salad with Indian spices

Feeds 6

1 x 400g tin chickpeas, drained and rinsed
2 ripe mangoes, peeled and cut into 1cm dice
3 small Lebanese cucumbers, or 1 large cucumber, peeled, cut in half lengthways, seeded and cut into 1cm dice
200g cherry tomatoes, quartered
1 small bunch mint, roughly chopped
1 small red onion, sliced into thin rounds
1 bird's eye chilli, finely chopped
Juice of 2 lemons
2 tsp sumac
1 tsp sugar
1 tbsp garam masala (page 166)
4 tbsp vegetable oil

Leave the rinsed chickpeas in a sieve whilst you make the salad and pat dry in a bundle of kitchen paper when you are ready to fry them.

Mix the mango and cucumber in a bowl with the tomatoes, mint, red onion and chilli and dress with half the lemon juice, the sumac, sugar and garam masala.

Chill the salad in the fridge and allow the flavours to gel whilst you fry the chickpeas. Heat a wide-bottomed frying pan over a high heat and when really hot add the oil. Now add the chickpeas and stir fairly continuously for about 7–8 minutes until they are golden and crispy all over. Beware, they are badly behaved and tend to spit and jump out of the pan if you don't keep stirring. Season generously with sea salt and toss into the salad. Now season the salad with more sea salt, tasting to check and adding the juice of the second lemon if the flavours need to be brighter. Serve alone or with little bits of crisp, baked pitta.

Frying chickpeas brings out their nuttiness

Asparagus, asparagus! It is such a treat when the season is on us but such a fleeting one that I tend to overindulge when it's finally here. This is my favourite way to eat it (perhaps vying with a plate of simply steamed spears with beurre noir or homemade hollandaise).

Chargrilled asparagus with salsa verde

Feeds 4

2 large bunches asparagus (or more if you are feeling greedy), woody ends snapped off
A large handful each of parsley and coriander, roughly chopped
A small handful of mint leaves, roughly chopped
4 anchovies
1 tbsp capers
2 small garlic cloves (or 1 fat clove)
1 bird's eye chilli, chopped
1 tbsp red wine vinegar
200ml extra virgin olive oil

Heat a chargrill over a high flame for at least 5 minutes. When it is smoking hot, brush the spears with a little olive oil and chargrill on both sides for 3–5 minutes until tender with dark and chargrilled streaks across the stems. You need to chargrill them in one layer so you may have to do this in 2 batches, depending on the size of your grill.

Meanwhile, put the herbs, anchovies, capers, garlic, chilli and vinegar in a food processor and whizz to a paste. With the motor running, slowly drip the oil through the funnel of the food processor until you have a thick sauce. Taste and adjust the seasoning. It will need a good pinch of salt and plenty of freshly ground black pepper. Serve the asparagus spears drizzled with the vivid green salsa verde and with fresh bread to mop it all up.

Tip – *Salsa verde is delicious with all kinds of fresh herbs: basil, coriander, mint, chervil and parsley work well in most combinations, so mix it up and see what you like best.*

These simple pots of cheesy, ethereal fluffiness make a great starter when you really want to push the boat out. They can be prepared in advance and popped in the oven after your guests have arrived to show off your cool-headedness. The slightly smoky, nutty crunch of the crust is irresistible.

Twice-baked goat's cheese and fennel soufflé with hazelnut crust

Feeds 8

You will need 8 small ramekins or dariole moulds

50g hazelnuts
1 tsp cayenne pepper
1 tsp sweet smoked paprika
80g butter
1 large fennel bulb, trimmed, finely chopped
60g plain flour
350ml warm milk
1–2 tbsp fresh thyme leaves
100g rindless soft goat's cheese
50g Parmesan cheese, freshly grated
4 eggs, separated
300ml double cream
Baby gem salad leaves, to serve
1–2 tbsp hazelnut or olive oil
Juice of ½ lemon

Preheat the oven to 190°C/375°F/gas 5. Toast the hazelnuts in the oven until light golden. Roughly chop half the nuts and set aside. Put the rest in a food processor with half the cayenne, some salt and the paprika, whizz to a paste.

Melt the butter in a saucepan over a low heat. Brush the inside of the moulds with a little of the melted butter then coat with the powdered nuts. Continue heating the remaining butter and when sizzling, add the fennel and sweat over a medium heat for 10 minutes until soft.

Turn up the heat, add the flour and cook for a few minutes, stirring all the time. Add the milk, little by little, stirring to create a creamy sauce. Add the thyme, goat's cheese and half the Parmesan and season with salt, black pepper and the rest of the cayenne. Remove from the heat and cool slightly before beating in 3 of the egg yolks to get a smooth, thick sauce.

Whisk the egg whites in clean bowl until they hold their shape. Carefully fold half the whites into the sauce, then fold in the rest. Stand the ramekins in a deep baking tray and fill the tray with boiling water half way up the moulds. Bake for 20 minutes until risen, golden and set.

Remove from the oven and leave to stand for a few minutes. Allow to cool (they will collapse at this stage but will rise again splendidly with the second baking), cover with cling film and chill.

Pour the cream into a small, heavy-based pan and season generously. Bring to the boil over a medium-low heat and simmer until reduced by at least half to a thick, pale yellow cream.

When ready, preheat the oven to 200°C/390°F/gas 6. Run a palette knife around the moulds and turn the soufflés out onto a baking tray, spaced a few centimetres apart. Spoon over the cream and sprinkle with the remaining Parmesan. Bake for 10 minutes until puffed up and golden. Serve with a baby gem salad dressed with oil and lemon juice, the chopped hazelnuts and a dusting of the powdered nuts.

Light, fresh and full of flavour, this is one of those salads that you build into your repertoire and keep coming back to. It works in the summer when you can roast corn on the barbecue and then shave off the kernels into the salad, and it works throughout the year with frozen corn. Go easy on the habanero – it's feisty stuff!

Corn, fennel, rocket and avocado salad

Feeds 6

1 tbsp oil
300g fresh or frozen sweetcorn kernels, or 2 large corn on the cobs
1 medium fennel bulb, trimmed and finely sliced
1 avocado, peeled, de-stoned and diced
½ red onion, very finely sliced
A large handful of rocket leaves
½ head of Cos lettuce or 1 orange, segmented
A handful of mint leaves

For the dressing
1 small habanero chilli
2 tsp cumin seeds
1 fat garlic clove
2 tsp soft brown sugar
1½ tbsp red wine vinegar
90ml extra virgin olive oil

To make the dressing, heat a dry frying pan over a high heat and add the chilli. Roast on all sides for about 10 minutes until it is charred and blackened all over. Add the cumin seeds towards the end and toast them for 1–2 minutes until they smell fragrant. Tip the cumin seeds into a pestle and mortar. Then, very carefully, as it is ferociously hot, cut open the chilli and scrape away the seeds and inside membrane. Cut up the remaining flesh and add a third to the pestle along with the garlic, sugar and a few good pinches of sea salt. Grind everything to a paste and add a little more chilli if you like.

You will probably only use half the chilli or the dressing will be extremely hot!

Mix in the vinegar, stir to dissolve the sugar and salt and finally stir in the oil. Check for seasoning, you may need a touch more salt.

Put the frying pan back over a high heat and when smoking hot add the tablespoon of oil, followed by the sweetcorn. Stir-fry the corn until slightly coloured on all sides, about 6–7 minutes. Season well with salt and pepper. Alternatively, roast the corn on the cobs over a barbecue for 10 minutes and cut away the corn after roasting.

Put all the salad ingredients into a large bowl, season with salt and pepper and dress with the habanero dressing. Serve at once.

Tip – *Frozen corn is an amazing product. Corn, like peas and broad beans, starts turning sugars to starch as soon as it is picked. Freezing arrests this process and stops the kernels turning horribly starchy – it's so much better than anything you'll find in a can.*

This is one of the most delicious recipes I have created and it really doesn't take much time to make. I use it for really special occasions, knowing that it will thrill friends and also involve me in no last-minute work – you can prepare everything in advance then sear the scallops at the last minute.

Caramelised scallop, avocado and orange salad

Feeds 6

4 small garlic cloves, peeled
2 tsp coriander seeds, toasted
2 tsp cumin seeds, toasted
1 chile de árbol
1 tsp salt, plus extra
6 tbsp olive oil
18 scallops, cleaned and trimmed
2 avocados, peeled, de-stoned and
  cut into quarters
Juice of 1 lemon
3 oranges
½ tsp sugar
3 heads of chicory or Castelfranco
  radicchio, broken up into leaves
1 bunch coriander, leaves only,
  roughly chopped

Crush the peeled garlic, spices and chilli with half a teaspoon of sea salt in a pestle and mortar. Pound together with 4 tablespoons of the olive oil. Marinate the scallops in half the spice mix for at least an hour.

Meanwhile, cut each avocado quarter into 2–3 slices. Squeeze over the lemon juice and season with salt and pepper. Peel and segment the oranges by cutting away the tops and bottoms and cutting each orange segment out from between the membrane. Squeeze the membranes to get as much of the juice as possible. Whisk 2 tablespoons of olive oil into the orange juice and add the remaining spice mix and the sugar. Check for seasoning.

Heat a frying pan over a high heat until smoking hot, then sauté the scallops, 6 at a time, for 3–4 minutes the first side and a minute or two on the second side until they are looking caramelised and delicious.

Gently mix the salad leaves, orange segments and scallops together in a large bowl with the dressing. Arrange the salad on a large plate, top with the avocado and chopped coriander and dive in.

These are inspired by Sabina Bandera's incredible sea urchin tostadas that I tasted at a food festival in Oaxaca. Bandera's street food stand, La Guerrense, in Ensenada is spoken of in hushed tones by Mexican food enthusiasts – it is famous throughout the Americas – and when I tasted these, I understood why. The combination of toasted peanuts, hot peanut oil, creamy avocado and seafood is inspired.

Prawn tostadas with avocado and spicy peanut oil

Feeds 4–6

250ml olive oil or vegetable oil, for frying
8 large corn tortillas
40g peanuts
1 large onion, peeled and finely sliced
Juice of 1 (juicy) lime
1 avocado
2–3 tbsp hot and fiery peanut oil (page 163)
150g (MSC certified) raw prawns
2–3 tbsp mayonnaise
2 baby gem, cut into fine ribbons
Hot sauce, for splashing (optional – see Tip)

Heat 250ml of oil in a small saucepan until it is shimmering hot. Meanwhile, cut out small circles from the tortillas, keeping the off-cuts to fry for salads or snacks, and test one in the hot oil. If the oil bubbles up vigorously, then it is up to temperature. If the oil doesn't move very much, wait for the temperature to rise further.

Fry the tortillas in batches so that you are not bringing the temperature of the oil down too much, until crisp and golden. Drain the tostadas on kitchen paper. Reserve the oil.

Heat a frying pan over a medium heat and toast the peanuts for about 5 minutes until pale golden all over. Remove them and roughly chop. Add a few tablespoons of the frying oil to the pan, followed by the onion and a good pinch of salt, and cook over a medium heat for about 10 minutes until the onion is soft and sweet-tasting.

All of this prep can be done a couple of hours in advance. Remove and set aside.

When you are ready to eat, peel, de-stone and cut the avocado into quarters, then squeeze over the juice of half the lime. Heat the frying pan again and when it is smoking hot add a few splashes of the peanut oil followed by the prawns. Toss the prawns in the oil for a few minutes until they have turned from translucent to pink. Add the onions, most of the rest of the oil and the nuts and briefly stir to heat through. You do not want to overcook the prawns. Squeeze the rest of the lime juice over the prawns.

Serve the tostadas with a smear of mayonnaise, the shredded lettuce, prawns and onion and top with the peanuts, avocado slices and more peanut oil drizzled over, scooping some of the delicious sediment from the bottom of the bottle over the prawns.

Tip – *Sabina serves these with a roast habanero sauce. Try the Wahaca one or scatter over a tiny pinch of de-seeded and finely chopped habanero chillies if you are a glutton for heat.*

scatter over a tiny pinch of de-seeded
finely chopped Habanero chillies if
you are a glutton for heat.

This Asian dish is a classic for a reason. The tingling effect of citrusy Sichuan pepper combined with the salty heat of the chillies enhances the sweet taste of the squid with its tender morsels of meat. It makes a brilliantly quick starter for those who like their flavours bold. I simply love it.

Salt and pepper squid

Feeds 4

500g small squid, cleaned and cut into generous bite-size pieces
2 tbsp sherry (preferably a medium dry like manzanilla)
4 spring onions, finely sliced on the bias
4 garlic cloves
1–2 fresh red chillies
2 tsp Sichuan pepper
2–3 tbsp vegetable oil
A handful of coriander leaves, roughly chopped
1 lime, half cut into wedges

Marinate the squid in the sherry whilst you finely slice the spring onions, garlic and chillies.

Put a dry wok over a very gentle heat and add the Sichuan pepper, stirring for a few minutes until the pepper smells wonderfully fragrant. Be careful not to burn it. Tip the pepper out into a pestle and mortar and grind to a fine powder. Sift the powder through a fine sieve, discarding the white husks that remain. The powder that sifts through is your roast Sichuan pepper.

When you are ready to eat, drain the squid (reserving the sherry) and season well with salt. Put the wok over a high heat and when it is smoking hot, add 2 tablespoons of vegetable oil. Throw in half the squid with a good sprinkling of the Sichuan pepper and stir-fry for 1–2 minutes until opaque and turning golden in places. Cooking them so briefly ensures that they stay tender. Repeat with the second half of the squid, allowing the pan to heat up again before adding more oil to the pan and sprinkling with more pepper.

Turn the heat down to medium, add a final tablespoon of oil and stir-fry the spring onions, garlic and chillies until the garlic starts to turn a pale golden. Now put the squid back into the pan with the strained sherry, the chopped coriander and the juice of half a lime. Toss to heat through and serve immediately with the lime wedges.

Tip – *This works just as well as a main course, served with rice, stir-fried beansprouts and broccoli.*

Skye Gyngell put a version of this on the menu when I worked at Petersham Nurseries. Back then its Asian flavours were completely new to me and I would marvel at how such a simple dish with so few basic ingredients could take the flavour of crab and make it sing. Hot, sour, sweet and savoury, this is one plate of food that I will never tire of.

Thai crab salad with Nam Jim dressing

Feeds 6

2 Lebanese cucumbers (or 1 regular, small cucumber), peeled, cut in half lengthways, seeded and peeled into ribbons
1 pink grapefruit, peeled and cut into segments
4 handfuls of pea shoots or watercress
1 handful of mint, leaves only
1 handful of Thai basil, leaves only
600g fresh crabmeat (2 dressed crabs)
1 lime, cut into wedges

For the Nam Jim dressing
2 garlic cloves, roughly chopped
6 coriander roots and stems, washed thoroughly, roughly chopped
1 bird's eye chilli, roughly chopped
2 tbsp soft, light brown sugar
2 tbsp fish sauce
juice of 2–3 limes (4 tbsp)

To prepare the dressing, place the garlic and coriander in a pestle and mortar with a good pinch of sea salt. Pound together until it resembles a green purée. Add the chilli to the paste and continue to pound. When it is fully incorporated, mash in the sugar and fish sauce. Season with the lime juice, adding a little at a time and tasting as you do so – you want a balance of sweetness, saltiness and sourness.

Place the ribbons of cucumber and the grapefruit segments in a large salad bowl, add the salad leaves and herbs. Lightly dress with about a third of the Nam Jim dressing. In another bowl, lightly dress the crabmeat with another third of the dressing.

Divide the salad between the plates and top with the crabmeat. Sprinkle the remainder of the Nam Jim over the salads and serve with a wedge of lime. If you like you can garnish the salad with crispy, fried shallots.

Black pudding has quite a butch reputation, but I adore it. The delicate sweetness of the roast pears, offset by the subtly smoky paprika, gives it a softer edge whilst the bitter, peppery taste of the leaves gives the salad lightness and crunch. I eat this often for lunch and sometimes give it to friends as a light starter.

Black pudding and chicory salad with roast pear and paprika

Feeds 4–6

3 ripe pears, quartered and cored
3–4 tbsp olive oil
1½ tsp sweet smoked paprika
A good pinch of caster sugar
150g green beans, topped and tailed
300g black pudding, sliced into 2cm coins
½ tsp hot smoked paprika
2–3 heads of chicory (red if you can get it), leaves separated
2 large handfuls of watercress

for the dressing
75ml extra virgin olive oil
2 tbsp red wine vinegar
4 tsp Dijon mustard
2 tsp honey
2 small shallots or 1 large, finely sliced

Preheat the oven to 220°C/430°F/gas 7.

Drizzle the pears in 2 tablespoons of olive oil and a teaspoon of the sweet paprika. Season with the sugar, salt and pepper and roast in the oven for about 20 minutes until they are tender throughout, a little browned on the edges but not collapsed.

Meanwhile, to prepare the dressing, mix the oil, vinegar, mustard and honey in an old, clean jam jar. Add the shallots and leave for a good half hour, to soften any acidic flavours.

Heat a small pan of water and when at a rolling boil, simmer the green beans for about 4 minutes or until just cooked but still with a little bite. Run under cold water to stop them cooking and drain.

Toss the black pudding in the remaining sweet smoked paprika and the hot paprika, then fry in a tablespoon of oil for a few minutes on each side until nicely browned and crisp. Drain on kitchen paper.

Toss the chicory leaves and watercress together with the green beans in a third of the dressing. Top with the pears and black pudding, drizzle with the rest of the dressing and serve whilst the pears and pudding are still warm.

2

Quick Fixes

When I get home from work late (and invariably tired) I like to have a few recipes up my sleeve that can be prepared and cooked with a minimum of fuss and in very little time.

These recipes are for the evenings when a takeaway is the other, more expensive option, except that it fills the kitchen with greasy packaging and is never quite as good as it promises. They are for the times when you want home-cooked food without the cooking, a fast food fix without the rubbish, a collection of failsafe recipes that will be simple, satisfying and a darn sight healthier and cheaper than anything you can pick up from the local Chinese.

This might be the time to turn to the lip-tingling tofu and broccoli stir-fry for a healthy start to the week, or the gently spiced, fried mushrooms on toast for something quick and moreish, or even the stir-fried salmon with its addictively spicy seed mix (that can be scattered on almost anything to good effect).

If you've thought ahead, you might have picked up some fresh mackerel on the way home – ten minutes in the oven and you have an aromatic, roasted wonder-fish, heady with its Goan spicing; or you might have the ingredients for the mouth-watering chicken-fried rice which can wear a hundred different guises depending on what's in the fridge and how much chilli you crave.

If famished, cook some pasta and perhaps toss it with the spiced pumpkin seed pesto, inspired by my travels in Mexico; or the fast and summery cherry tomato, black olive and garlicky breadcrumbs, tossed raw into hot pasta for a warm and wonderfully juicy sauce that you know is doing you the world of good.

These are the recipes that you can learn by heart and rustle up in a moment. When my family is clamouring for food, sometimes weary, sometimes cross, sometimes just plain hungry, I know that these recipes will create a contented buzz around the table.

It's hard to express how much I like mushrooms on toast. I'm talking about masses of sautéed garlic, lots of extra virgin olive oil, a good dose of butter and plenty of time for those mushrooms to fry. Even accounting for lots and lots of time in the pan, this supper dish can be made in about 20 minutes, making it one of my favourite, fast turnaround suppers.

Gently spiced mushrooms on toast

Feeds 6

40g butter
3–4 tbsp extra virgin olive oil, for cooking
6 fat garlic cloves, finely chopped
1 chile de árbol, torn into tiny pieces
1kg Portobello and chestnut mushrooms, finely sliced
100ml single cream
A large handful of parsley, roughly chopped
4 thick slices of sourdough bread
A really good extra virgin olive oil, for drizzling

Heat a large frying pan over a high heat and when hot add the butter and oil. Throw in the garlic and chilli and stir with a wooden spoon for a minute or two until the garlic is just turning a pale golden. It is very important not to burn the garlic so watch that it doesn't turn a dark brown; the moment it is golden throw in the mushrooms.

Turn the heat down to medium and cook the mushrooms, stirring from time to time, for about 15 minutes, seasoning them generously with salt and pepper. They will first turn golden in the hot fat and then they will start to release all their water. By the end of cooking the water will have evaporated leaving richly flavoured, soft mushrooms that are not remotely watery (a curse for good mushroom flavour). Add the cream and parsley, cook for another few minutes so that the cream has bubbled down and enveloped the mushrooms.

Toast the bread, rubbing the slices with the remaining clove of garlic and drizzling with your best extra virgin olive oil. Top with the mushrooms, season with one final slick of oil and serve.

Tip – *I always have a bottle of non-supermarket label, new season, deep green olive oil in my cupboard for a dish like this; it has the potential to transform an ordinary dinner into something bloody brilliant!*

Pumpkin seeds are an important source of protein and good essential oils, and have long been a staple of Mexican cuisine: the Aztecs and Mixtecs would grind them down with spices and chillies to make rich, exotic sauces. This is my simple version; it works beautifully with pasta and is also delicious with grilled chicken or poussin.

Linguine with a deliciously spicy pumpkin seed pesto

Feeds 4

1 large, very ripe tomato
3 garlic cloves, skins on
1 habanero/Scotch bonnet chilli
75g pumpkin seeds
1 tbsp fresh oregano leaves
a large handful of coriander leaves, roughly chopped
1 tsp salt
1 small shallot, peeled and roughly chopped
70g pecorino, freshly grated, plus more for serving
Juice and zest of ½ lime
Juice and zest of ½ orange
120ml extra virgin olive oil
300g linguine

Heat a large, heavy-bottomed frying pan over a high heat. Place the whole tomato, garlic cloves and chilli in the pan and dry roast until they are blackened, blistered and soft. The tomato will take a little longer, so fish out the garlic and chilli first as they are cooked (about 5–10 minutes). Slip the skins off the garlic cloves and cut the chilli in half, removing and discarding the stem, seeds and inner veins.

Meanwhile, toast the pumpkin seeds in another dry frying pan until they become toasted all over and start to 'pop'. Blitz the pumpkin seeds with the herbs and salt in a food processor and then add the tomato, garlic, chilli, shallot and pecorino and blitz again. Finally add the citrus juices, zest and olive oil and blitz to a pesto.

Cook the pasta until al dente in plenty of well-salted boiling water and drain, reserving the cooking water. Toss the pasta with the pesto, followed by 2–3 tablespoons of the reserved cooking water. Allow to sit for a minute or two and add a few tablespoons more water if needed to loosen the pasta. This stops it from becoming dry when you get it to the table. Serve with lots of freshly grated pecorino and, if you like, a green salad.

Toast the pumpkin seeds until
they start to 'pop'

I am not usually prescriptive about what type of pasta to buy but in this recipe the brown nuttiness of wholewheat penne goes brilliantly with the spicy, sweet-savouriness of the cauliflower, raisins and nuts. This is a really great dish to rustle up on a dull weekday evening – it is packed with flavour but takes very little time to make and is proof that a cauliflower can do more than hide behind cheese (although I like it doing that too – see page 148).

Penne with fried cauliflower, raisins and pine nuts

Feeds 4

1 whole cauliflower, cut into 3–4cm florets
5 tbsp olive oil
1 tsp caster sugar
50g raisins
1 tsp crushed fennel seeds
2 chiles de árbol, finely chopped
1 large onion, finely chopped
2 garlic cloves, chopped
150ml white wine
320g wholewheat penne
30g pine nuts, toasted
A handful of chopped parsley
50–60g pecorino, freshly grated

Bring a large pan of water to the boil. Add the florets and simmer for a few minutes, just enough to get rid of their hardcore crunch. Using a slotted spoon, transfer the cauliflower to a sieve, keeping the water in the pan for the pasta.

In a wide-bottomed frying pan, heat 2 tablespoons of the oil and when hot add the cauliflower and a teaspoon of sugar. Fry over a high heat for about 5 minutes, turning the florets until they are coloured on all sides. Now turn the heat right down, add another 2 tablespoons olive oil, the raisins, crushed fennel seeds, chilli and onion. Cook for another 5 minutes, stirring once, add the garlic and continue to cook for another few minutes until the onion is soft and translucent. Now add the wine, turn up the heat a little and simmer until the wine is thick and syrupy.

Meanwhile bring the cauliflower water back to a vigorous boil, add the pasta and cook until al dente. Drain the pasta, reserving half a cup of pasta water.

Toss the pasta in the cauliflower, then drizzle with the remaining olive oil and scatter with the pine nuts, parsley and grated pecorino. If it looks a little dry, moisten with a touch of the cooking water. Check for seasoning and eat at once.

Tip – *Try this with grilled sardines instead of cauliflower – it works a treat.*

*This is one of my favourite summer pasta recipes, more like a fresh dressing than a pasta sauce
and harnessing all the delightfully sunny flavours of ripe tomatoes, basil and fennel seeds.
The warm tomato juices combine with the bitter notes of a good extra virgin olive oil and black
olives; soft, yielding pasta and crunchy, garlicky breadcrumbs finish off the plate. A glass of chilled
dry white wine, sunshine and friends are all that's needed to complete the picture.*

Orecchiette with cherry tomatoes, black olives and toasted breadcrumbs

Feeds 4

600g cherry tomatoes
100g Kalamata or other black olives, stone-in
2 garlic cloves
1 tsp sea salt
1–2 pinches of sugar
8 tbsp extra virgin olive oil
½ tsp fennel seeds, ground
1 chile de árbol, seeds removed and crumbled
100g breadcrumbs
A large handful of basil, de-stemmed
  and shredded
300g orecchiette or other scoop-shaped pasta

Roughly chop the tomatoes, keeping every bit of juice and seeds that you can. Smash the olives with the flat of your chopping knife, discard the stones and roughly chop. Put the olives in a bowl with the tomatoes. Crush the garlic to a paste with a pinch of salt and add half to the tomatoes along with at least a teaspoon of sea salt, plenty of black pepper and the sugar to taste. Pour in 5 tablespoons of the olive oil and leave to steep for at least 10 minutes (but no longer than an hour), to allow the flavours to develop.

Heat the remaining oil in a frying pan and add the rest of the garlic paste. Cook over a medium heat for a minute or two before adding the fennel seeds, chilli and breadcrumbs. Fry for 5–10 minutes until the crumbs are toasted and golden. If you like, add a pinch of sugar (I do). Remove to a bowl.

Finally, cook the pasta in plenty of well-salted boiling water. Transfer the tomatoes to the frying pan that you cooked the crumbs in and place on top of the pan of water so that the sauce gets a chance to warm through (alternatively place the tomatoes over a low heat). You don't want to cook the sauce, just warm it.

Once the pasta is al dente, drain, keeping back a few tablespoons of the cooking water. Toss the pasta in the tomatoes, basil, crumbs and cooking water. Check for seasoning and serve at once.

Tip – *The quality of the black olives is key here: forget about buying a tin of stoned olives; instead seek out the soft, squidgy stone-in Kalamata olives from good deli counters.*

I never used to be a fan of tofu, I just didn't get the fuss over an ingredient that seemed to spend its time floating around in water. But then I delved further into Asian cuisine and realised what a versatile, healthy ingredient it is and how well it soaks up flavours. This hot, fragrant stir-fry is one of the yummiest, fast weekday suppers that I have in my repertoire. I prepare all the vegetables beforehand and then toss them together in a wok at the last minute.

Spicy Sichuan noodles with tofu and broccoli

Feeds 4

1 small head of broccoli
200g firm, fresh tofu, cut into 2cm cubes
1 tsp Sichuan pepper
200g egg noodles
3 tbsp sesame oil
3 tbsp vegetable oil
3 garlic cloves, finely chopped
1 large knob of ginger, peeled and finely chopped
1–2 Sichuan chillies, seeds removed and torn into pieces
1–2 tbsp Chilli oil (see page 163)
2 tbsp Sichuan chilli bean paste (see page 21)
6 spring onions, trimmed, sliced 2cm thick on the bias
1 red pepper, de-seeded and finely sliced
2 tbsp soy sauce
a good pinch of sugar

Cut each of the broccoli florets down the centre into quarters and peel the stalk, cutting it into small fingers. Cover the tofu with boiling water and leave to soak for 10 minutes. Toast the Sichuan pepper in a dry frying pan for a few minutes until the pepper smells wonderfully fragrant. Be careful not to burn it. Tip the pepper out into a pestle and mortar and grind to a fine powder, then sift through a fine sieve, discarding the white husks that remain.

Cook the noodles according to the packet instructions then drain in cold water. Toss with enough sesame oil to coat the noodles.

Heat the vegetable oil in a medium-hot wok, then add the garlic, ginger, Sichuan chillies, chilli oil and chilli bean paste. Cook for a few minutes until you can really smell the aromatics, but without burning. Turn the heat right up, add the vegetables and stir-fry for 3–4 minutes. Now add the soy sauce, sugar and 100ml water.

Make a well in the middle and add the drained tofu. Gently cover the tofu in the vegetables and simmer for a few minutes to allow the vegetables to finish cooking and the tofu to absorb all the delicious flavours. Sprinkle with the Sichuan pepper and serve over the noodles.

Tip – *If you have a good deli or Asian grocer, get the fresh tofu that's set in a tub.*

oast the Sichuan pepper in a dry frying pan for a few minutes until the pepper smells wonderfully fragrant.

The melding together of sweet squash and crunchy amaretti, tender sheets of pasta, a bite of chilli and the earthy notes of nutmeg and sage produces a sophisticated little number. This recipe may be easy but its decadent texture and taste mean that I am as likely to give it to friends coming over as I am to cook it for an indulgent, cosy night in.

Cheat's pumpkin ravioli

Feeds 4

1 medium acorn squash, peeled, de-seeded and cut into 3–4cm cubes
90ml extra virgin olive oil
2 fat garlic cloves, finely chopped
1 chile de árbol, finely chopped
80g Parmesan cheese, grated
1 tsp balsamic vinegar
A grating of nutmeg, to taste
12 lasagna sheets (about 375g)
120g butter
30 sage leaves
15–20g amaretti biscuits, crushed

Bring a pan of water to the boil, add the squash and simmer for 10–15 minutes until just cooked through. Drain.

Warm half the oil in a large saucepan over a medium heat and add the garlic and chilli. Cook for a few minutes until the garlic has softened (but before it has started to darken in colour). Stir in the squash and cook for about 5–10 minutes over a low heat so that the squash begins to break up into a rough pulp. Season with half the grated Parmesan, the balsamic vinegar and a good grating of nutmeg, along with plenty of salt and freshly ground black pepper. Set aside for when you are ready to eat.

When you are ready to eat, bring a large pan of well-salted water to a rolling boil and add the lasagna sheets. Meanwhile melt the butter in a pan, season well with salt and pepper and when sizzling add the sage leaves. Cook until the butter starts to darken and the leaves start to turn crisp. Remove from the heat.

Cook the pasta until al dente, drain, cut the sheets in half to make smallish squares and drizzle with a little oil. Sprinkle a dusting of amaretti on 4 serving plates followed by a layer of pasta. Top with an eighth of the squash purée, a good drizzle of sage butter, a dusting of amaretti and another pasta square. Repeat finishing with the third pasta square. Top with the last of the butter, a good grinding of black pepper, the rest of the grated Parmesan, and a final flourish of olive oil.

My dear friend Lucy, who is a wonderfully inventive cook, gave this recipe to me. It's a simple and delicious dish, with a delicate blend of flavours that suits a complex Chardonnay or a flinty Meursault, and hungry friends!

Spaghetti with lemon, anchovy, spinach and capers

Feeds 4

3 very ripe beef tomatoes
2 tbsp olive oil
3 fat garlic cloves, finely chopped
10 anchovies
1–2 fresh red chillies, finely chopped
300g spaghetti
6 tbsp extra virgin olive oil
50g capers
Zest and juice of 1 lemon
400g spinach
A large handful of basil, shredded
A large chunk of Parmesan cheese, to serve

Pour boiling water over the tomatoes, count to 30 and drain. Peel the tomatoes and roughly chop the flesh, seeds and all. Put a large pan of well-salted water onto the boil.

Heat a large, deep frying pan or casserole dish over a medium flame. Add the (non virgin) olive oil, turn down the heat a touch and when the oil is warm add the garlic, anchovies and chilli. Sauté gently in the oil using a wooden spoon to break up the anchovies so that they 'melt' into the sauce; be careful not to cook over too high a heat or the garlic will burn. Cook the spaghetti in the boiling water.

When the garlic is soft and slightly creamier in colour add the capers, tomatoes, zest and lemon juice. Turn the heat up a notch and allow the sauce to simmer for a minute or two before adding the spinach in 3 lots, stirring between each addition to wilt the spinach down and create space in the pan to add more. Throw the shredded basil over the spinach, and add the extra virgin olive oi. Season with plenty of freshly ground black pepper and perhaps a touch of salt.

Once the spaghetti is cooked, pour over the lemon and caper sauce and eat at once, with a grater and a large chunk of Parmesan to hand around the table.

There is something about the flavour of mackerel that works beautifully with rich, sensual Indian spices. This is what we often have for Sunday night suppers when I have been to the market, bought some blisteringly fresh mackerel and want supper on the table in a jiffy. I like to serve the spice-infused fish with some boiled waxy potatoes tossed in mounds of butter.

Goan-spiced mackerel

Feeds 4

1 scant tbsp cardamom pods
2 tsp cumin seeds
2 tsp fennel seeds
1 tbsp coriander seeds
1–2 chiles de árbol, according to taste
  or 2 tbsp garam masala (page 166)
½ tsp black peppercorns
5 tbsp vegetable oil, plus extra for drizzling
1 medium onion, finely chopped
3 garlic cloves, finely chopped
2–3cm knob of ginger, peeled and
  finely chopped
1½ tsp turmeric
2 tbsp tomato purée
4 mackerel, scaled and gutted
1 lemon, cut into wedges

Preheat the oven to 200°C/390°F/gas 6.

Gently bash the cardamom pods in a pestle and mortar (or with the side of a big knife) and pick out the little black seeds. Discard the green husks.

Put the cardamom seeds, cumin, fennel, coriander, chile de árbol and peppercorns in a dry frying pan and warm for a few minutes over a medium-hot flame. Transfer to your pestle and mortar (or a spice grinder) and grind to a fine powder.

Heat the oil in the same frying pan and add the onion. Cook for 10 minutes or until the onion is soft and translucent, then add the garlic, ginger, turmeric and spices. Stir-fry for a few minutes before adding the tomato purée and salt to taste, stirring again and removing from heat.

Cut the mackerel on each side with about 3 deep gashes, place them in a baking dish and rub them thoroughly with the spice paste, inside and out. Drizzle with a little extra oil and roast for 10 minutes. Serve with wedges of lemon and some boiled waxy potatoes.

This recipe is thanks to my daughter, Tati. Wanting to feed her something healthy and delicious, I steamed greens from the fridge, cooked some noodles and then threw in all the ingredients I had lying around. The Spiced seeds were sitting temptingly on the side – she insisted on throwing them in. The scant amount of salmon stretches amazingly well, making it an affordable, healthy supper dish I would happily eat every week.

Easy-peasy salmon and spring green stir-fry

Feeds 4

350g spring greens, tough stems removed, cut into 2–3cm ribbons
1 large organic or wild salmon fillet (about 250g)
2–3 tbsp sesame oil
2 chiles de árbol, torn in half
1 large onion, finely chopped
3 fat garlic cloves, finely sliced
5cm knob of ginger, peeled and finely chopped
3–4 tbsp soy sauce
3 tbsp sherry
A good handful of Spiced seeds (optional, see page 164) or some toasted sesame seeds

Wash the spring greens in plenty of cold water and then place in a large pan over a medium heat. The residual water will provide enough moisture to steam cook them, about 4–5 minutes with occasional stirring. Once wilted down and tender turn off the heat and set aside. Cut the salmon fillet into thick slices and each slice in half.

Now put a large wok over a medium-high flame and add 2 tablespoons of sesame oil followed by the chilli. Stir-fry for a minute or two to flavour the oil and fry the chilli until it blackens a little, then add the onion, garlic and ginger. Stir-fry, stirring continuously, until the onions have softened and turned translucent. Turn up the heat, add another splash of oil and the salmon and stir-fry for a minute or two until the salmon pieces have started to colour. Now add the greens, soy sauce and sherry and stir for another minute or two to heat through the greens. Scatter with the Spiced seeds or toasted sesame seeds.

Tip – *I usually eat this with noodles that I cook in advance, rinse under cold running water (to prevent the noodles sticking together) and then toss through the stir-fry to heat up at the last minute, but it is equally good with rice.*

Fried rice is beloved of toddlers, teenagers and grown-ups alike for its comforting nature and savoury taste. Follow the simple guide below or get creative, using leftovers in the fridge or strange ingredients lurking in the cupboard: slivers of pork, beef and fish are all good, as are prawns and peas, broccoli, sweetcorn and shiitake mushrooms. In this version, the smoked oysters (which you can buy in tins from most good supermarkets) add a heady smoky flavour to the dish.

Super-fast chicken-fried rice

Feeds 2

3 garlic cloves, peeled
2–3 tbsp Thai chilli jam (see page 178)
  or 1 tbsp Thai red curry paste (page 21)
1 tbsp light soy sauce
1 tbsp oyster sauce
7 tbsp vegetable oil
200g leftover chicken, shredded or
  roughly chopped
2 eggs
320g cooked basmati rice
  (equivalent to 100g uncooked)
½ tsp white sugar
4 spring onions, trimmed and finely chopped
1 small bunch coriander, roughly chopped
60g smoked oysters (optional), halved
1 lime

Mash the garlic in a pestle and mortar with a pinch of salt. Mix the Thai chilli jam (or curry paste) in a bowl with the soy and oyster sauce.

Heat 4 tablespoons of the oil in a large wok over a medium heat and when hot add the garlic and cook for a few minutes, stirring, until it is golden. Scoop out with a slotted spoon and transfer to a large bowl. Add the chicken and stir-fry for a few minutes to heat up, then transfer to the same bowl.

Now turn the heat right up and when the oil is hot break in the eggs. Once the whites have started to brown on the outsides scramble the eggs with your spoon. When they are cooked but not before add another tablespoon of oil and the rice. Now stir-fry for a few minutes then add the chilli jam-soy mix and the sugar. Stir a few times before throwing the chicken and garlic back in, together with the spring onion, coriander and oysters, if using. Squeeze over half the lime, stir and check for seasoning. You may want an extra few teaspoons of soy sauce.

Serve at once with wedges of the second half of lime, and cucumber slices.

Tip – *If you are feeding more than 2, simply prepare double the ingredients and cook in two batches.*

Guide
Whilst fried rice is fast to cook it is also easy to mess up. Here are four rules you should stick to:

1. *Use leftover rice; if you need to cook it fresh, use a little less water than usual.*
2. *Make sure the rice is at room temperature when you cook it – you want the grains neither too hard nor too soft.*
3. *Use plenty of oil. You are not going to be eating a mass of meat so do not fret about the fat.*
4. *Prepare all the ingredients first so that you can cook it all in a flash.*

This fast stir-fry is adapted from a recipe in David Thompson's incredible book, Thai Food. *I have dramatically reduced the amount of chillies in my version. David may be the only person I would fear in a chilli-off. This is a great way to do something different with the mince sitting in your fridge. Serve with rice and a fried egg on top, or a bowl of fish sauce seasoned with finely sliced shallots, garlic and a squeeze of lime juice, to complete the Thai experience.*

Stir-fried minced beef with Thai basil

Feeds 4

2 fresh red chillies, de-stemmed, de-seeded and roughly chopped
3 garlic cloves, peeled
4 bird's eye chillies, de-stemmed, de-seeded and roughly chopped
3 tbsp vegetable oil or lard
600g minced beef
150ml beef or chicken stock, or water
1 tsp caster sugar
½ tbsp each light and dark soy sauce
1 large bunch Thai basil (see Tip), stalks discarded, leaves roughly shredded

Tip the chillies, garlic and a large pinch of salt into a pestle and mortar and grind to a paste.

Heat a wok over a very high heat and add the oil (or lard), followed by the chilli paste. Stir-fry for a minute before adding the mince bit by bit and continuing to stir-fry for a few minutes, breaking up the meat with a spoon.

Pour in the stock, sugar and soy sauce, heat through for a few minutes, to finish cooking the meat, then turn off the heat and check for seasoning. If you use stock rather than water you will need less soy sauce. If you think it needs more seasoning add a dash more soy sauce. Stir in the fresh herbs and serve at once over rice. I love Thai Fragrant – about 75g per head should be plenty.

Tip – *If you can't get hold of Thai basil, the aniseed flavours of tarragon along with our European basil makes a good substitute, or use a bunch each of normal basil and coriander.*

3

Soups and other one pots

Whilst I do love to go for it when cooking, during the week I am often (always) short of time and that's when I want to be able to throw a few ingredients into a pot and have a great plate of food emerge the other end, without having to spend hours washing up a load of pans. Soups and other one pots are the perfect solution to this – a neat way to cook delicious, reviving food without working too hard.

Soups in themselves are ingenious at packing your body with all the goodness that vegetables and a great stock provide, without you having to slave too long over a hot stove. They are comforting in their essence (picture yourself clutching a hot cup of soup on a cold winter's evening), easy to prepare and really do make you feel good. The vibrantly hot and sour Chicken, coconut and lemongrass soup will blow out the cobwebs like nothing else; for something a little more hearty try the Tuscan chickpea and vegetable soup with its touch of chilli heat. My mother's amazing Beetroot, parsnip and horseradish soup never fails to make me feel restored and re-energised with its sweet, spicy and earthy warmth.

Sometimes something more substantial is needed that still won't leave the kitchen piled high. How about a richly seasoned Sausage and radicchio risotto or an aromatic Spanish fish stew with a wonderfully spicy almond crumb? Or for something healthy and vibrant an Indian mussel rasam or the gloriously spicy Chicken piri piri? These are dishes designed to leave you with very little washing up, dishes that will feed you well without breaking the bank. I hope you find them as useful as I do.

I first tasted this gazpacho in Oaxaca, Mexico, at the amazing food festival that takes place there every September. Chefs from all over Mexico fly in and show off their regional cooking; this soup was made by Diego Hernandez, a talented chef from Baja California, who made the simplest ingredients hum with flavour. It is the most vivid emerald green and makes a delicate, beautiful and unusual starter.

Creamy green gazpacho
with spinach and avocado

Feeds 6, as a starter

50g almonds
500g spinach
1 banana shallot, peeled and roughly chopped
4 tbsp best-quality extra virgin olive oil
A large handful each of basil and chervil,
  roughly chopped
Juice of 2 limes
6 cherry tomatoes, halved
2–3 ripe mixed tomatoes, cut into wedges
1 fresh red chilli, de-seeded (if you like) and
  finely chopped
1 ripe avocado, peeled, de-stoned and cut into
  small dice or thin wedges
A handful of fresh, peeled raw (or just cooked)
  broad beans (optional)

Heat a frying pan over a medium heat and slowly toast the almonds for 5–10 minutes, tossing fairly often until pale gold (if the heat is too high the almonds will burn in places). Roughly chop.

Heat a large pan of water and when boiling add the spinach and shallot and cook for 1–2 minutes until the leaves have wilted. Drain the spinach, reserving about 200ml of the cooking water, and rinse under running water until cool (cooling it down quickly keeps the spinach's vivid green colour).

Put the spinach and shallot in a food processor with 4 tablespoons of the olive oil, the reserved cooking water, the basil and chervil (reserving some for the garnish) and a good few pinches of salt and whizz into a paste. Cover the soup well and leave to chill for a few hours in the fridge.

When you are ready to eat, season the soup with more salt and pepper as needed, and the lime juice (if you add it sooner it can make the soup turn a sludgy green). Pour the soup into shallow bowls and decorate with the tomatoes, chilli, the rest of the oil, avocado, almonds, broad beans and a scattering of the fresh herbs. It is also lovely scattered with any edible flowers you may have growing on herbs and salad leaves. Serve at once.

Tip – *I only decorate with beans if they are very fresh, or with young fresh peas which are a lovely garnish with a sprinkling of pea shoots.*

Also lovely with any edible flowers
you may have growing or herbs
and salad leaves

Cauliflowers make the smoothest, creamiest soups and avocados make the smoothest, creamiest salsas. Here the two ingredients complement one another, with the silky avocado mixed with sweet, crunchy hazelnuts and fresh lime to soften and add sparkle to the toasty, gentle heat of the chilli and the earthy coriander. A simple, satisfying and unusual starter or supper dish.

Spiced cauliflower soup with avocado salsa

Feeds 4

2 tbsp olive oil
1 onion, diced
2 sticks celery, finely sliced
½ tsp Turkish chilli flakes, plus more to garnish
1 tsp coriander seeds, crushed
2 garlic cloves, chopped
1 medium floury potato, peeled and diced
1 large head of cauliflower, broken up into large florets
1 litre vegetable stock or water

For the salsa
1 large, ripe Hass avocado, peeled, de-stoned and diced
25g hazelnuts, toasted and roughly chopped
Juice of 1 lime
2 spring onions, finely diced
2 tbsp olive oil
1 small bunch coriander, roughly chopped

Heat a large saucepan or casserole dish, pour in the olive oil, then add the onion, celery, chilli and coriander seeds. Season to taste then cook, stirring occasionally, for about 10 minutes until the onion has turned silky soft and translucent. Add the garlic and potato and cook for a further few minutes, stirring to coat the potato in oil before finally adding the cauliflower and enough stock or water to cover.

Simmer the broth until the cauliflower is completely tender. Whizz up with a stick blender and taste to check the seasoning, adding more salt and pepper if you think it needs it.

Stir all the salsa ingredients together and season to taste. Serve the creamy soup with dollops of the fresh, zingy salsa on top and a scattering of chilli flakes, if you like.

You can buy lemongrass and lime leaves from most good supermarkets and they freeze well; the lime leaves will keep fine in a sealed bag and the lemongrass is best whizzed to a paste in a food processor then stored in an airtight pot. Alternatively, you could replace these ingredients with a dollop of Thai curry paste (see page 21). This winter warmer is extremely easy to make and deliciously fragrant with all its Thai spicing.

Thai style spicy pumpkin soup

Feeds 4

3 tbsp vegetable oil
1 medium onion, finely chopped
1 heart of celery, trimmed and chopped
1 small bunch coriander, stalks finely chopped,
  leaves roughly chopped
5 Kaffir lime leaves
2 sticks lemongrass, finely chopped
3 garlic cloves
1 bird's eye chilli, de-stemmed
1.2kg pumpkin, peeled and cut into
  chunks (see Tip)
1.2 litres chicken stock or water
150ml coconut milk
A drizzle of chilli oil (optional, see page 163)

Heat a large pan over a medium heat and add the oil. When hot, add the onions and celery, season well with salt and pepper and cook until the vegetables are soft and translucent, about 10 minutes.

Add the coriander stalks, along with the lime leaves, lemongrass, garlic and chilli. Sweat with the onion and celery for another 5 minutes before adding the pumpkin. Stir the pumpkin briefly to coat in the oil and then pour over enough stock or water to cover the vegetables. Simmer for about 20–25 minutes until the pumpkin is completely soft.

Blitz the soup with a stick blender and pour it back into the pan over a low heat, stirring in the coconut milk and allowing it to heat through for a few minutes. Serve, scattered with the roughly chopped coriander leaves and, if you love heat, a drizzle of chilli oil (see page 163).

Tip – *If you can't get hold of pumpkin use a largeish butternut squash or 2 acorn squash instead. You may need a little more liquid in the soup, but otherwise cook it just the same.*

This is a wonderfully comforting soup that I often make in the winter as the vegetables are usually lying around in my fridge and I always have chickpeas in the cupboard. It is so easy to make – just remember, when dicing and slicing the vegetables, to try to keep them all roughly the same size, about 1cm dice.

Tuscan chickpea and vegetable soup

Feeds 4

120ml extra virgin olive oil
2 sticks celery, finely sliced
½ large fennel bulb, trimmed and diced
1 medium onion, diced
2 carrots, peeled and diced
5 fat garlic cloves, sliced
1 chile de árbol, crumbled
2–3 bay leaves, preferably fresh
1 sprig of rosemary, leaves picked and finely chopped
½ Savoy cabbage, cored and sliced thinly
400g cooked chickpeas (see Tip)
Slices of thick, crusty bread
1 garlic clove, cut in half
Parmesan cheese, freshly grated, to serve

Heat a large casserole dish over a medium heat and when hot add the oil followed immediately by the celery, fennel, onion, carrot, garlic, chilli and herbs. Season generously with sea salt and freshly ground black pepper and cook the vegetables over a medium heat for 25–30 minutes until they are totally soft and transparent, without colouring. You may need to add a splash more olive oil during the cooking.

Add the cabbage and chickpeas and pour in 1.2 litres of water. Bring up to simmering point, then leave to simmer gently for 15–20 minutes until the cabbage is tender. Check for seasoning and add more salt and pepper if needed. If you can, allow the soup to sit overnight; the flavour will improve dramatically.

When you're ready to eat, toast the bread on a chargrill or in a toaster and rub the cut side of the garlic all over it.

Serve the hot soup in preheated bowls drizzled with generous spoonfuls of extra virgin olive oil, lots of freshly grated Parmesan cheese and the garlic toast to dip.

Tip – *The supermarkets now sell cooked chickpeas in cartons – they are much larger and softer than the ones in tins, which tend to be like hard little bullets unless you find the Napolina brand. You can also buy good cooked chickpeas in large glass jars from Spanish delis, but these are quite a bit more expensive.*

This is one of those soups that you will find yourself coming back to again and again: undeniably healthy and blissfully easy to make. The flavour combination of the sweet, earthy beetroot, the fiery fresh ginger and the bite of chilli and horseradish is extraordinary, so I take my hat off to my mother for discovering such a delicious combination. Make this with the best chicken stock and horseradish that you can muster – it will make all the difference.

My mother's amazing beetroot, parsnip and horseradish soup

Feeds 4

3–4 tbsp olive oil
1 large onion, finely chopped
450g raw beetroot, peeled and cut into 2–3 cm chunks (wear gloves to avoid neon pink fingers for the rest of the day)
3 large parsnips (about 450g), peeled and cut into 2–3cm chunks
1 heaped tbsp grated ginger
1 tsp freshly grated horseradish or 2 tsp horseradish sauce (see Tip)
1 chile de árbol, de-seeded
1.25 litres chicken stock
100ml single or double cream
A small handful of chives (optional)

Heat the olive oil in a large pan over a medium heat. Add the onion, season well with salt and pepper and cook for about 10 minutes, until completely soft and translucent. Add the beetroot, parsnip, ginger and horseradish and crumble in half the chilli (or more if you like it spicy). Add another splash of oil if you think the mixture looks dry and cook, stirring occasionally, for another 5 minutes before pouring in the stock.

Bring to the boil and cook until the vegetables are completely tender. Whizz with a stick blender, check the seasoning and serve with a small pool of cream in the middle and, if you like, a scattering of finely chopped chives.

Tips – *If you are in a hurry, chop the vegetables into smaller pieces and they will cook much more quickly.*

When buying horseradish sauce check the back of the bottle – a good-quality one will be packed with horseradish and taste good and fiery; a bad one will contain very little horseradish and will taste vinegary and bland.

Rasam is a fresh, aromatic soup from Southern India, made with tomatoes, chillies and spices. You should have most of the spices already but if not visit an Asian supermarket and stock up. I go easy on the chillies here so their heat doesn't detract from the overall taste.

Southern Indian rasam soup with mussels

Feeds 4

2 tbsp split yellow lentils (optional, see Tip)
1kg mussels
½ tsp cumin seeds
1 tbsp coriander seeds
½ tsp peppercorns
1 chile de árbol
4 garlic cloves
½ tsp turmeric
1 bunch coriander, stalks and leaves separated and finely chopped
3 tbsp vegetable oil or ghee
2 x 400g tins plum tomatoes
½ tsp mustard seeds
A pinch of sugar
½ tsp mustard seeds
A few sprigs of fresh curry leaves (optional)

Wash the lentils in cold water, cover with a litre of water and bring up to simmering point. Simmer gently for 20 minutes and drain, reserving the cooking water. Meanwhile clean the mussels, tearing away their beards and checking that they are alive by tapping sharply. If they stay open, they are dead and need to be thrown; if they shut they are good.

Gently toast the cumin, coriander, pepper and chilli in a dry frying pan over a medium heat for a few minutes until you can smell their oils. Grind them to a powder in a pestle and mortar or spice grinder and then add the garlic, turmeric and coriander and pound to a paste.

Heat a third of the oil in a large, roomy pan over a high heat and when smoking hot add the cleaned mussels and a small ladle of the lentil cooking water. Close the lid and steam cook for a few minutes, shaking vigorously a few times until the mussels have opened, about 5 minutes. Discard any that remain shut. Pour through a sieve, preferably lined with muslin (which removes any nasty grit) and set aside.

Wipe out the pan and heat another third of the oil then add the spice paste. Cook over a medium heat for a few minutes, stirring, before adding the tomatoes, a good half teaspoon of salt and a pinch of sugar. Cook for 5–10 minutes before adding the rest of the stock from the lentils. Mash the lentils in the pestle and mortar and add them too.

Add the mussels and their cooking liquor back into the soup and scatter with the coriander leaves. Check for seasoning, adding more salt if you like. Finally, heat the remaining oil in a small saucepan and when smoking hot throw in the mustard seeds and curry leaves, if using, and after a minute pour the whole lot into the broth. Ladle out into warmed bowls and serve.

Tip – *Split yellow lentils are easy to find in supermarkets but if you can't get hold of them simply use water instead of the lentil stock.*

Last year, just before the birth of our second child, I went to Thailand and Cambodia to try the food in its proper setting. I was blown away by the clarity, freshness and lightness of the flavours – and by how much of the food I could eat. This soup was a particular favourite, so easy to make but so, so good. It is amazingly healthy!

Chicken, coconut and lemongrass soup

Feeds 4

2 banana shallots, finely sliced

2 sticks lemongrass, cut into 5cm pieces and
  bashed with the flat of a knife

8–10 Kaffir lime leaves

10 thin slices of ginger

1.2 litres vegetable or chicken stock

200g chestnut or shiitake mushrooms, brushed
  clean and cut in half

400g skinless chicken thighs or breasts, sliced
  into 2–3cm thick pieces

2 bird's eye chillies, finely sliced

150g peas

300ml coconut milk

Juice of 2–3 juicy limes

3 tsp caster sugar

3–4 tbsp fish sauce

Put the shallots, lemongrass, lime leaves, ginger and stock in a saucepan and bring to the boil. Turn down the heat and simmer gently for 5 minutes before adding the mushrooms, chicken, chillies, peas and coconut milk.

Bring to the boil again and simmer for 3–4 minutes until the chicken pieces have turned a creamy white colour and are no longer at all translucent. If in doubt, fish one out to check.

Add the lime juice, sugar and fish sauce, stir and try a mouthful of the broth, adding salt to taste. Eat at once.

Tip – *Don't be afraid of seasoning this soup properly with both fish sauce and salt. If you add both seasonings little by little, tasting as you go, you will find the magic umami balance – it makes all the difference to the final taste.*

Fish stew is one of those failsafe dishes that I cook often. It always reminds me of a weekend in Spain when we went out with some local fishermen and caught enough to feed 40 which we cooked in an old beaten-up tin barrel. I have added a crumb to this version, as it lifts the stew from a cosy old supper dish into something altogether more glamorous. Make it your own by using your favourite type of fish and, if you like, add shellfish for more body.

A simple Spanish fish stew with an almond crumb

Feeds 4

4 tbsp olive oil
2 medium onions, finely chopped
1 medium fennel bulb, trimmed and
  finely chopped
4 garlic cloves, sliced
2 tsp fennel seeds, roughly ground
1 chile de árbol
2 good pinches of saffron strands
3 garlic cloves, finely chopped
2 x 400g tins plum tomatoes
500ml water or fish stock
600g new potatoes, cut into 2–3cm chunks
900g line-caught cod, cut into large
  2 inch chunks

For the almonds
100g blanched almonds
1 tsp sweet smoked paprika
1 tsp sea salt

Preheat the oven to 180°C/350°F/gas 4.

Heat a large casserole dish over a high heat and when hot add the olive oil. Turn the heat down to medium before adding the onions, fennel, garlic, fennel seeds, chilli and saffron, and seasoning generously with salt and black pepper. Sweat the vegetables in the olive oil for 10 minutes before adding the garlic and cooking for another 5 minutes. Add the tomatoes, breaking them up with a wooden spoon, then pour in the water or stock and the new potatoes. Check for seasoning.

Simmer the stew for about 20–25 minutes, or until the potatoes offer up no resistance when you push a sharp knife through: they should be completely cooked. In the meantime, put the almonds on a baking tray and pop in the oven for 5–10 minutes until a pale golden colour. Roughly chop with a large chopping knife to make fairly coarse breadcrumbs and stir in the paprika and salt.

Add the fish to the stew once the potatoes are cooked and simmer for a further 5 minutes until the fish turns from translucent to opaque. Spoon into hot bowls and sprinkle over the almond crumbs.

This is a simple recipe inspired by grilled chicken you find in my neighbourhood. I wanted to create an easy home-cooked chicken dish with that addictive, splendidly fiery flavour. There is no nonsense to this recipe: just whizz up the marinade, let it sit overnight and then throw it all in one pan. The result is sweet, citrusy, delicious and hot; perfect for a weekday supper.

Chicken piri piri with new potatoes, red peppers, oregano and lemon

Feeds 4

8 chicken thighs
3 tbsp olive oil
2 large shallots, sliced
4 red peppers, seeds removed, roughly sliced
600g new potatoes, roughly halved or quartered
½ lemon, thinly sliced
A good splash of red wine or water
(about 30ml)

For the marinade
5 fat garlic cloves
3 bird's eye chillies, stalks removed
but seeds left in
2 tbsp pomegranate molasses
2 tsp mustard powder
1½ tbsp tomato purée
Juice of ½ lemon
1 tbsp red wine vinegar
1 tbsp Worcestershire sauce
A small handful of fresh oregano, leaves
picked and roughly chopped

For the marinage, place all the ingredients into a blender and whizz to a purée, seasoning with a few good pinches of sea salt. Slash the flesh of the chicken pieces a couple of times and then pour the marinade over them. Allow to marinate for at least a few hours or overnight.

Preheat the oven to 200°C/390°F/gas 6.

Heat a large casserole dish over a medium-high heat and when hot add a few tablespoons of olive oil followed by the shallots, peppers, new potatoes and lemon. Toss them around and season well. When the shallots have become translucent add another splash of olive oil and the wine (or water) and bring back to the boil. Place in the oven and roast for half an hour, uncovered.

Now add the chicken pieces, nestling them in the dish skin side up. Cook for another 30–35 minutes, or until the chicken is just cooked and golden on top. Serve at once, with buttery rice or sweetcorn.

If you think that a bowl of soupy risotto richly seasoned with red wine, Parmesan and garlicky sausage meat sounds like heaven then this is the recipe for you. It makes a great dinner for friends with a green salad and is easy peasy to make.

Risotto with chilli, radicchio and sausage

Feeds 4 hungry people

600ml good red wine
600ml chicken stock
4 fat Toulouse or Italian spiced sausages
3 tbsp olive oil
1 medium onion, finely chopped
40g butter
2 small heads of radicchio or Treviso (or ½ small Savoy cabbage), finely shredded
1 tbsp good-quality balsamic vinegar
2 fresh red chillies, de-seeded and finely chopped
3 garlic cloves, finely chopped
1 small bunch thyme, leaves stripped
300g Arborio or other short grain risotto rice
50g Parmesan cheese, finely grated

Heat the wine and stock together over a gentle flame and keep warm over the lowest heat ready for the risotto. Squeeze the meat out of the sausage skins.

Heat the oil in a large, heavy-bottomed pan then add the sausage meat, using a wooden spoon to mash the meat as it cooks, breaking it down into little chunks. Cook until golden brown, then add the onion and cook for 5–10 minutes.

Meanwhile, in a separate pan, heat half the butter and when sizzling hot add the shredded radicchio. Stir-fry for 5 minutes until wilted, then sprinkle over the balsamic vinegar.

Once the onions are soft, stir in the chilli, garlic and thyme. After a minute add the rice and stir for a few minutes to thoroughly coat the grains in fat. Now add a ladleful of the wine stock and stir into the rice until it has been completely absorbed.

Keep adding the liquid, stirring continuously, almost beating the mixture with a wooden spoon as if you were lightly whipping cream. After about 15 minutes stir in the sautéed radicchio; after another 10 minutes, when the liquid has been used up the rice should be tender but still with a slight bite to it.

Season with salt and pepper, stir in the remaining butter and some Parmesan cheese and check again for seasoning. Serve at once with a good bottle of medium-bodied red wine and more Parmesan to serve.

4

From the
Store Cupboard

I learnt to cook at my mother's side, playing around with whatever ingredients I could find lurking in the fridge or in the corners of the cupboards. Now that I work, and am a mother myself, I finally understand the fallback position you can reach, cooking the same collection of safe, workable dishes over and over again. It is hard enough getting home to feed, bathe and bed the babies without having to think of something interesting to cook for dinner.

If one is clever, one dinner works for everyone – especially if children have grown up a little and are adventurous with food – but the trick is dreaming up something that is both simple and quick to prepare with supplies that you already have in the house. As a child, without the responsibility of cooking on my shoulders, I found this an edifying challenge, infinitely more appealing than homework. I would spend hours with my nose buried deep in my parents' cookbooks, conjuring up fantastical food combinations until I found something that fitted the bill and could be finished in time for supper. I became hooked on the praise and the good will that I could garner from these efforts: there was a fair amount of anxiety and tension in those days but a carefully prepared plate of food could somehow leave us feeling a little more alive, possibly even pleased to be around.

This training stood me in excellent stead, for this was store cupboard cooking at its best. So get into the recesses of your cupboards, pull out some ingredients and be inspired. Make the simple but exquisite potato, pea and ginger curry, a failsafe recipe to give you the buzz that curries always do, or the baked potatoes stuffed with a rude-boy, all-American chilli beef, or a plate of your own Homemade baked beans (always, always a winner with boys). With a little time you could be feasting on an oozing rarebit sandwich; or some seriously yummy, silken aubergine dressed in a garlicky, chilli, ginger sauce; or the consoling Almond, apricot and carrot pilau, delicious on its own, even better with grilled chops or sausages. Never let your imagination hold you back; your cupboards and their contents are the doors to a brave new world of cooking.

These are the most delicious morsels of toasted cheesy wonder. I like to serve them with a green salad for supper, but cut into quarters or tiny squares they make a delectable nibble when friends pay you a surprise visit. Just whack them out on a big wooden board and people will be swooning with delight. It is important to make the mix at least an hour before you want to eat so that it has a chance to set.

Welsh rarebit and leek sandwiches

Feeds 4 for a hearty supper
or 8–10 for rustic canapés

20g butter
2 tbsp plain flour
1 tsp English mustard powder
1 tsp cayenne pepper
A good splash of Worcestershire sauce
220ml strong ale
500g extra mature Cheddar
2 medium leeks
1 sourdough loaf, cut into thin slices

Melt the butter in a heavy-bottomed pan and, when sizzling, stir in the flour and cook for a few minutes until it smells toasted but hasn't browned. Add the mustard powder, cayenne pepper and Worcestershire sauce before stirring in the ale, bit by bit. Add the cheese and stir to melt until you have a smooth, fairly thick sauce.

Pour the sauce into a shallow container and transfer to the fridge or freezer to set. You want it to be a completely firm paste the texture of playdough by the time you are ready to cook.

Meanwhile, clean the leeks under running water, trim and slice into thin (½ cm) rounds. Simmer them in boiling water for a few minutes until soft, then drain, pushing out any excess water. Season well with salt and pepper.

When you are ready to eat, scoop out some cheese mix (kids love doing this bit) and mould into a paddle the same shape as the bread slices and about ½–1cm thick, depending on how greedy you feel.

Spread the outsides of the bread slices with butter, fill the sandwich with the cheese paddles and a layer of leeks. Toast in a toasted sandwich maker or fry on both sides over a low heat so that the cheese melts as the bread browns. I like to press the sandwiches gently with a fish slice so that the cheese oozes out and fries crisp and golden on the bottom. Cut into halves and serve with a green salad, or into small squares, if you have a crowd to feed.

Tip – *Any leftover cheese mix lasts well in the fridge for a week and freezes brilliantly. It is also delicious spiked with either a tablespoon of chipotles en adobo (page 169) or Thai chilli jam (page 178) so experiment with your chillies! For meat lovers, take out the leeks and add some slices of prosciutto or cured ham instead.*

Delicious spiked with a tablespoon of chipotle adobo or Thai chilli jam!

I love potatoes, I love peas and I love curry. This combination of all three is just right for satisfying a deep and gnawing hunger. I can wolf down a couple of pittas stuffed with this simple vegetarian curry in one sitting, especially when it's dressed with a good mango chutney and plenty of raita. It is the perfect TV dinner and soul food for those who love a tingle on their lips!

Pittas stuffed with potato, pea and ginger curry

Feeds 6

800g floury potatoes, peeled and cut into rough
  2cm chunks
1 tsp fenugreek seeds
1 tsp coriander seeds
2 tsp cumin seeds
½ tsp nigella seeds
1 chile de árbol, or 2 if you like it hot
1 large knob of ginger, peeled and cut into
  chunks
4 tbsp vegetable oil
1 medium onion, finely chopped
1 tsp turmeric powder
1 x 400g tin plum tomatoes
250g fresh or frozen peas
1 tsp salt, to taste
A pinch of sugar, to taste
Toasted pitta bread, to serve

Boil the potatoes in salted water for 15–20 minutes or until tender. When cooked through drain in a colander or sieve and leave to steam-dry whilst you toast the spices.

Meanwhile, warm a dry frying pan over a medium heat. Put the fenugreek, coriander, cumin, nigella seeds and dried chilli in the pan and toast over a medium heat for a few minutes, just long enough to unlock the spices' fragrance. Grind them in a spice grinder or pestle and mortar and set aside. Blend the ginger to a paste with 4 tablespoons of water.

Heat a pan over a medium-high heat and when hot add the oil, followed by the onion, the spice mix and the turmeric. Turn the heat to medium and fry for 5 minutes, stirring occasionally, to soften the onion. Add the ginger water and continue to cook for another 5 minutes until the onion is soft.

Add the potatoes, tomatoes and peas and 100ml water and cook for about 15 minutes to coat the potatoes in the tomato sauce, seasoning with at least 1 teaspoon of salt, some freshly ground pepper and a pinch of sugar to taste.

Serve the potato curry in toasted pitta bread with big leaves of Cos lettuce, some Coriander raita (see page 172) or cooling plain yoghurt and mango chutney. Yum!

There are variations of this dish throughout Turkey, Northern Africa, the Middle East and Spain: no wonder, as it's such an easy, quick fix and so resuscitating when you are feeling done in. In Spain, the eggs are served with a sprinkle of sweet smoked paprika; in the Middle East, with sumac and melted butter; in Turkey, with dollops of creamy labneh (a delicious strained yoghurt) and rich, smoky Turkish chilli flakes. Cook it your own way – it's great with garlic-rubbed toast on the side.

Turkish eggs

Feeds 4

4 tbsp olive oil
2 medium onions, finely chopped
1 red pepper, de-seeded and diced
1 tsp cumin seeds, ground
4 garlic cloves, crushed
2 tbsp harissa (page 167), optional
2 x 400g tins plum tomatoes
a good pinch of brown sugar
8 eggs
A small bunch of coriander, roughly chopped
Turkish chilli flakes, to sprinkle (optional)
Greek yoghurt or labneh, to serve

Preheat the oven to 180°C/350°F/gas 4.

Heat a deep, wide frying pan or a casserole dish with ovenproof handles, then add the oil. Once the oil is warm, turn the heat to a medium flame and add the onions, pepper and cumin. Cook for at least 10 minutes until the onions have turned soft and translucent. Add the garlic and harissa and cook for a further 5 minutes before adding the tomatoes and sugar and seasoning well with salt and pepper.

Break up the plum tomatoes with a wooden spoon and cook the sauce on a gentle simmer for 10 minutes to allow the flavours to meld, checking for seasoning and adding more salt, pepper, harissa or sugar if you think it needs it.

Now make 8 little pools in the sauce and into each pool break an egg. Try to stir the whites into the sauce a little without breaking the yolks. Bake in the oven for 5–10 minutes until the yolks are just cooked, but still runny, and serve scattered with the coriander and, if you like, a dusting of Turkish chilli flakes. Serve with Greek yoghurt or Labneh.

Tip – *If you don't have harissa, use sweet and hot smoked paprika in the base instead or sprinkle more chilli flakes on at the end.*

I used to make these for my housemates in Mexico City – they were always a big hit. Homemade baked beans are infinitely better than tinned and go brilliantly with toast, poached eggs, a plate of sautéed greens, or just on their own, when the cupboard is bare. Tone the chipotle up or down depending on who you're cooking for – the recipe below has a lovely smoky kick to it. Oh, and if you make them in advance, the flavour improves immeasurably after a day or two.

Homemade baked beans

Feeds 6

**350g dried haricot beans plus 1 whole
  head of garlic or 3 x 400g tins haricot
  beans, drained and rinsed**
5 bay leaves
2 tbsp olive oil
1 medium onion, chopped
3 garlic cloves, finely chopped
2 sticks celery, finely chopped
100g streaky bacon, chopped
1 tsp dried oregano
1 tbsp chipotles en adobo (page 169)
1 x 400g tin plum tomatoes, chopped
2 tsp Worcestershire sauce
2 tbsp maple syrup

If you are cooking your own beans cover them with at least 3cm of water, add the head of garlic, cut in half horizontally, and 2 bay leaves. Cook for 1–2 hours until tender.

Preheat the oven to 190°C/375°F/gas 5.

Heat the oil in a large heavy-bottomed casserole dish over a medium heat. Sauté the onion, garlic, celery and bacon until the onion has softened, about 10 minutes. Add the rest of the bay leaves, the oregano and chilli and sweat for a further 2–3 minutes before throwing in the rest of the ingredients. Season to taste.

If you are using tinned beans, add them to the pan now with 250ml water and bring up to simmering point. If you have made your own throw them in and only add a cup of water if the beans look dry (you will probably not need to). Cover with a lid and put in the oven for 1 hour or until the beans are juicy but not swimming around in liquid.

Store in a cool part of the kitchen overnight and eat the next day, if you can wait.

Tip – *I like to cook the beans myself as they are always much more tender and fully flavoured but tinned works fine if I am whipping this together when I get home from work. The recipe makes lots, as it's so moreish you'll want some leftover – it lasts for up to a week in the fridge and is great with eggs, in pasta, or added to mince.*

This is one of those suppers that I keep coming back to, especially in the depths of winter. The combination of spinach, sage and the deliciously nutty brown butter is the perfect foil for some fast cooked potatoes and a tin of beans. And the hint of cayenne livens everything up. The sauce is also amazing over homemade gnocchi.

Borlotti beans with spinach, sage, burnt butter and cayenne

Feeds 4

700g floury spuds, peeled and cut into bite-sized pieces
2 x 400g tins borlotti beans, drained and rinsed
120g butter
½ tsp cayenne pepper
A good grating of nutmeg
20 sage leaves (plus a few fried sage leaves to garnish, if you like)
125g mascarpone cheese
2 eggs
300g spinach
40g Parmesan cheese, finely grated

Put the potatoes in a pan of well-salted water, bring to the boil and cook until almost tender. Drain then return to the pan together with the borlotti beans and set aside.

Meanwhile, melt the butter in a small pan and season generously with salt, cayenne pepper and a good grinding of nutmeg. Cook over a high heat until the butter foams up and starts to form smaller, calmer bubbles on the surface. Once you start smelling that wonderful nutty aroma and the milk solids on the bottom of the pan have browned, remove from the heat and add the sage leaves which will sizzle in the hot fat. Be careful not to heat the butter too long after it starts browning or it will burn. Pour all but a tablespoon of the butter over the potatoes and beans and warm over a low heat.

Beat the mascarpone with the eggs and season well. Wash the spinach and shake briefly so that there is still some water clinging to the leaves. Wilt in a large saucepan with the remaining butter over a medium heat. Stir in the mascarpone mixture, warm through and then fold into the warm potatoes. Add the grated Parmesan, check for seasoning, then serve in warm bowls with a drizzle of olive oil and, if you like, a few crispy fried sage leaves to garnish.

Sichuan food has real character, with fierce heat, deep umami flavour and a wonderfully simple approach. Here, aubergines are roasted hot until soft and succulent and doused in a fragrant sauce of fried garlic, chilli and ginger. The result is a sensuous tasting dish, delicious with a bowl of nutty brown rice, or a decadent accompaniment to the duck on page 114 or the pork on page 117.

Sichuan aubergines with ginger, garlic and chilli

Feeds 4

4 large aubergines (about 1.2kg)
100ml vegetable oil

For the sauce
2 tsp cornflour
3 tbsp vegetable oil
2 tbsp Sichuan chilli bean paste (see page 21)
1 chile de árbol or 2 Sichuan chillies, crumbled
2cm knob of ginger, peeled and finely chopped
3 garlic cloves, finely chopped
250ml chicken or vegetable stock
2 tbsp dry sherry (Manzanilla is best, or fino)
1 tbsp brown rice vinegar
2 tbsp soft brown sugar
4 spring onions, finely sliced
1 small bunch coriander, roughly chopped

Cut the aubergines into rounds about 1–2cm thick and cut the rounds in half. Sprinkle them with a little fine sea salt and leave to drain in a colander in the sink or on the draining board for at least half an hour, to draw out any excess water.

Preheat the oven to 220°C/430°F/gas 7. When the aubergines are drained, toss them well in 100ml vegetable oil and roast in the oven for 30–40 minutes, until the aubergines are completely soft and a tempting golden on the outside.

Meanwhile, get the sauce ready. Mix the cornflour with 2 tablespoons of water. Heat the oil in a large wok and when hot add the chilli bean paste. As soon as it starts sizzling, add the chilli, ginger and garlic and stir-fry for a minute or two, taking care not to burn the chilli and garlic. If necessary take the wok off the heat for a few minutes or the sauce will taste bitter.

Pour in the stock and cornflour paste and cook for a few minutes to allow the sauce to thicken, then add the sherry, vinegar and sugar and simmer together for a few minutes to allow the flavours to meld.

Serve the aubergines on a heated plate with the sauce poured over and scattered with the spring onions and coriander. I love to serve this over bowls of steaming brown basmati rice for a healthy but decadent tasting supper.

This is a gloriously spiced dish and so satisfying to put together from bits and pieces in the cupboard. I have only added one chilli for a lovely background warmth, but if you want a little more bite, by all means add another, or use a good dollop of Harissa (see page 167) instead.

Almond, apricot and carrot pilau

Feeds 4–6

1 chile de árbol, de-seeded
2 tsp cumin seeds, ground
2 tsp allspice berries, ground
A large pinch of saffron
3 tbsp olive oil
40g butter
3 large onions, halved and finely sliced
100g dried apricots, roughly chopped
3 garlic cloves, roughly chopped
400g basmati rice, rinsed in cold water
Zest and juice of 1 lemon
150g carrots, peeled and cut into 1cm dice
60g blanched almonds, roughly chopped
150g cooked lentils (optional)
1 large bunch coriander, roughly chopped

Grind the chilli in a pestle and mortar with the cumin, allspice and saffron. Heat a large saucepan over a medium-high heat, add the olive oil and half the butter and when sizzling add the onions and apricots. Turn the heat down to medium and stir-fry for about 10 minutes until the onions have turned a wonderful nutty brown colour, without burning.

Add the garlic and spices, cook for a few minutes and then stir in the rice. Cook for a few more minutes to coat thoroughly in the fat and spices, adding more oil if the onions are sticking. Finally, add the zest and lemon juice along with 700ml cold water and bring the rice to simmering point. Simmer uncovered for 10 minutes then cover

with a lid, turn the heat to its lowest setting and continue to cook for another 5 minutes.

Meanwhile, melt the rest of the butter in a small saucepan and add the carrots. Season them with salt and pepper and stir-fry for a few minutes to colour. Transfer the carrots to a bowl and fry the almonds in the same fat over a very low heat until they have turned a light caramel colour. Add both to the rice, along with the cooked lentils, if using, and cook for another 5 minutes.

Take the rice off the heat and allow the steam to finish the cooking, which will take half an hour. Try not to stir the rice as this will make it stick together.

Scatter the pilau with masses of chopped coriander and serve as is for a simple supper.

Tip – *If you want to make this more substantial scatter with feta or sautéed shrimp. It is also delicious with the Middle Eastern lamb on page 120. I like to serve a bowl of garlicky yoghurt alongside, scattered with Turkish chilli flakes.*

Use a dollop of harissa for a little more bite

Sometimes when I get home in the evening all I want is a soothing and easy plate of vegetables – something that I can prepare without any faff. This recipe is a kind of rarified beans on toast, with lentils, instead of beans, cooked until soft and yielding and flavoured with the sweetness of stewed onions and fennel. Liven it up with a sprinkling of Turkish chilli flakes and mellow with a scoop of goat's cheese. Finally, eat with a spoon – perfect comfort food.

Falling apart lentils with sweet fennel

Feeds 4

4 tbsp extra virgin olive oil
a large knob of butter
1 large onion, finely diced
3 young fennel bulbs, trimmed and diced
A small handful of thyme sprigs
100ml dry white wine
175g Puy lentils
2 large handfuls of rocket
200g goat's curd (see Tip)
2 tbsp finely chopped parsley
1 tsp Turkish chilli flakes
extra virgin olive oil

Heat the olive oil and butter in a heavy-bottomed frying pan over a medium heat. When the fat has melted, add the onion, fennel and thyme, and season generously with salt and pepper. Cook gently for about 20 minutes until the vegetables are soft and translucent. Add the wine and simmer for a few minutes more.

Meanwhile, cover the lentils with plenty of water and season with salt. Bring to the boil and simmer them for 20–25 minutes until they are completely tender, then drain.

Stir the vegetables into the lentils then stir the rocket through. Spoon onto heated plates and top with dollops of the goat's curd, chopped parsley, chilli flakes and a slick of olive oil. If you're hungry, add some garlic-rubbed toast too.

Tip – *If you can't find goat's curd, crumble over some goat's cheese instead, or whip up goat's cheese with a couple of large tablespoons of crème fraiche to lighten both its flavour and texture.*

There are few sights more splendid than this dish of sautéed chicken livers, sweet onions, and steaming lentils and rice, topped with jewel-pink pomegranate seeds, paprika and green flecks of chopped coriander leaf. It is a homely, deeply restorative dish that takes very little time to make – luckily, as it seems to be a firm favourite in my house.

Warm spiced lentils and rice with chicken livers, lemon and pomegranate

Feeds 4

120g green or brown lentils
250g chicken livers
1 tsp ground cumin
40g butter
2 tbsp vegetable oil
2 onions, peeled, halved and finely sliced
½–1 tsp cayenne pepper
2 tsp sweet smoked paprika
Juice of 1 lemon

To serve
225g basmati rice, cooked
Seeds of 1 pomegranate
A small bunch of coriander, roughly chopped
A pinch of sweet smoked paprika

Rinse the lentils in cold water and pour in a saucepan. Cover with at least 3cm of cold water, bring to the boil, lower the heat and simmer until tender. (The cooking time will vary depending on what type of lentils you are using).

Meanwhile, sift through the livers with a sharp knife or pair of scissors, cutting out any bits of white gristle. Season them generously with salt and pepper and the ground cumin.

Heat a large frying pan over a high heat and, when the pan is smoking hot, add half the butter. Swirl the butter around the pan to melt it, then add half the livers and fry for about 30 seconds a side until they are brown and caramelised all over, then set aside. Repeat with the remaining livers.

Heat the same pan over a medium heat and add the oil and the rest of the butter. When the fat has melted, add the onions, cayenne and smoked paprika. Season with salt and pepper and cook for 15 minutes until the onions are sweet and soft.

Stir in the cooked lentils and lemon juice and check for seasoning. Finally, add the chicken livers and about 100ml water and heat through for about 5 minutes.

Serve the lentils over piles of steaming hot rice, sprinkled with the pomegranate seeds, coriander and a dusting of the sweet smoked paprika.

Tip – *This is wonderful with the Coriander raita on page 172.*

Stew onions in butter until
soft and sweet.

This is one of those incredibly simple recipes that I always turn to in the summer when I want to make something out of nothing. I like to wrap it in foil hot from the oven to take on a picnic: it seems to taste better warm than hot and with that flaky, buttery pastry, it's also delicious cold, served with a green salad and some boiled potatoes.

Roasted red pepper
and goat's cheese tart

Feeds 4

230g ready-made all-butter puff pastry
150g roasted red peppers
 (jarred to make it easy), cut into strips
½ red onion, finely sliced
12 cherry tomatoes, halved
25g pine nuts
80g goat's cheese, crumbled
½ tsp Turkish chilli flakes or a pinch of
 sweet smoked paprika

For the tapenade
1 garlic clove
Zest and juice of ½ lemon
1 tbsp of capers, washed in cold water
110g black olives
A good handful of basil leaves, roughly chopped
1 large fresh red chilli, roughly chopped
6 tbsp extra virgin olive oil

Preheat the oven to 220°C/430°F/gas 7.

To make the tapenade, whizz all the ingredients apart from the olive oil in a food processor until roughly combined, then add the olive oil.

Roll the pastry, place on a lined or buttered baking sheet and chill for 20 minutes. Lightly smear the base of the tart with the tapenade, making sure you leave a border of pastry, 1cm wide, all the way around.

Scatter the base with the strips of pepper, onion, tomatoes, pine nuts and cheese. Brush the edges of the pastry with a beaten egg and bake in the oven for 15 minutes or until the pastry has risen and is golden and crisp and the tomatoes and onion are cooked. Sprinkle with the chilli flakes and serve.

Tip – *Break a couple of eggs on top before baking if you want to make the tart a little more substantial.*

There is a reason why Sichuan cooking is world famous – the tongue-numbing, mouth-smarting combination of Sichuan pepper and chilli gives a chilli fiend such a profound rush that it is easy to see why chillies are considered to be addictive. In this easy recipe, adapted from one of Fuschia Dunlop's, the mix of garlicky, gingery chilli heat and citrusy-tingling pepper turns a simple chicken stir-fry into an intensely seasoned, deeply satisfying feast.

Spicy, fragrant chicken with chilli, ginger and peanuts

Feeds 4

You will need a large wok.

**4 chicken breasts (skin on or off),
 cut into 2cm cubes**
125g roast peanuts
70ml vegetable oil
**15 Sichuan or chile de árbol chillies,
 de-seeded, cut into 2cm pieces**
2 tsp Sichuan pepper
6 fat garlic cloves, sliced
**3–4cm knob of ginger, peeled
 and finely chopped**
**1 large bunch spring onions, top
 and tailed, cut into 2cm pieces**

For the marinade
1½ tbsp cornflour
2 tbsp dry sherry (fino or amontillado)
1 tsp salt
4 tsp good-quality light soy sauce

For the sauce
2 tbsp caster sugar
3 tbsp cornflour
1½ tbsp soy sauce
**2 tbsp brown rice vinegar
 (or regular rice wine vinegar)**
2 tsp sesame oil
250ml water or chicken stock

For the marinade, mix the cornflour with the sherry, then add the rest of the marinade ingredients and a couple of tablespoons of water. Add to a bowl with the chicken and set aside.

Mix the sauce ingredients together in a bowl. Heat a small frying pan over a medium heat and toast the peanuts, shaking the pan fairly regularly until they have turned a pale golden all over. Even if you buy ready roasted, toasting the peanuts hugely improves their flavour.

Heat your wok over a high flame and add the oil, chillies and Sichuan pepper and stir-fry for a minute or two until the chillies have darkened but not burnt (the chillies turn horribly bitter when they are burnt). Immediately add the chicken and stir-fry until the chicken pieces have separated from each other (initially they will stick together from the sticky marinade). Now add the garlic, ginger and spring onions and continue to cook until it smells delicious and the chicken pieces are cooked through.

Finally, stir the sauce then add it to the wok and stir to coat the chicken pieces. When the sauce becomes thick and syrupy add the peanuts. Serve at once with some greens and big bowls of brown rice to soak up the chilli heat.

Tip – *Instead of rice, try purple sprouting broccoli cut into finger-size pieces and tossed into the wok with the chicken.*

The first expression my husband tried to teach our eldest when she started talking was 'bad-ass'. I think of this recipe as bad-ass. The mince is cooked with an all-American cast of ingredients: ketchup, mustard, cumin and cayenne, and I think it is perfect to eat in front of a gangster movie – a kind of junk food fix without the junk. Use half the amount of cayenne if you are cooking for non-chilli lovers.

Baked potatoes with American chilli beef

Feeds 4

4 jacket potatoes
5 tbsp olive oil
1 heaped tbsp sea salt
1 tsp cayenne pepper
3 tsp ground cumin
2 tsp dried oregano
1 large Spanish onion, finely chopped
3 fat garlic cloves, finely chopped
500g minced beef
3 tbsp ketchup
1 tbsp Dijon mustard
Juice of 1 fat lime
About 20g butter
50g Cheddar cheese, grated
Everyday hot sauce (page 176), Wahaca's chile de árbol sauce or Tabasco, to serve

Preheat the oven to its highest setting. Pierce the potatoes through with a skewer about 5 or 6 times. Put them in a roasting tin and, donning a pair of washing-up gloves to keep your hands clean, rub with 1 tablespoon of the olive oil and a heaped tablespoon of sea salt. Bake for around 65–70 minutes until the skin is puffed up and crispy. Alternatively, put the potatoes into a microwave-safe bowl, cover with clingfilm and microwave on full power for 15 minutes before rubbing with the salt and oil and baking for a further 15–20 minutes (but this way you will forego that marvellous chewy skin, which is my favourite part of a baked potato).

Meanwhile, heat the remaining oil in a large frying pan or casserole dish and add the cayenne, cumin and oregano. Fry over a medium-high heat for a minute before adding the onion. Cook in the oil for 10–15 minutes until the onion has turned soft and translucent. Add the garlic and, after a minute, a third of the mince, breaking it up into tiny pieces with a wooden spoon. When the first lot of mince is ground down and browned, repeat the process for the last two-thirds. When all the mince is browned and looking crispy, add 200ml water along with the ketchup, mustard and lime juice. Simmer for 5 minutes to let all the flavours meld.

Cut each potato in half and add lashings of butter, a good grating of Cheddar and finally the mince. Douse with a chile de árbol or other hot sauce and serve with a crunchy slaw or a crispy green salad.

5

looking for
friends

When I think about friends coming for dinner – those times when the wine was flowing, the food felt good and people left laughing and happy in the small hours – my finest memories are never linked to hours spent slaving over a hot stove, getting into a panic about what to cook. The older I get the less time I spend worrying about what I'm going to cook and the more time I spend relishing the idea of putting certain ingredients together, of cooking a particular piece of meat or fish, creating a feast that will please me and hopefully therefore delight my friends.

I think the more fun you have preparing food the more rewarding the results. A happy cook makes happy food and happy guests. Who cares if you run out of time and are half way through cooking when everyone arrives? Get them chopping, washing, tossing and stirring with a drink in hand and you'll all have fun together.

Sometimes I am in a cosy mood and will make a simple supper and be done with it. When I have more time to shop I can do more, not just in terms of the time I can put into it but also in the effort of dreaming up delicious concoctions; such as the king prawns in spicy curry paste that was created from the memories of an incredible Cambodian beach holiday; or the Thai grilled beef, inspired by some seriously good street food in Bangkok.

The duck breast with caramel seven-spice sauce and the chicken schnitzel with its gloriously psychedelic tomato salad that screams of Mexico were similarly invented in my haphazard, magpie-like way; a memory here, an ingredient there, a moment of relaxation in some farflung place where I've loved the food has led me to a particular dish. This is the type of food that I want to shower on my friends.

When the first of the asparagus starts appearing it really is a sign that summer is around the corner. Next up are broad beans, young tender peas and delicious runner beans that barely make it to the pot, so delicious are they munched raw. This light stew is brimming with flavour from new season's garlic, young summery vegetables and a really good olive oil. I think it is one of the most delicious things you can eat, and to think that it is such a plateful of goodness to boot. Brilliant.

Broad bean, asparagus, fennel and green bean summer stew

Feeds 4–6

2 tsp fennel seeds
2 medium fennel bulbs, trimmed (reserve any leafy fronds)
3 tbsp best quality extra virgin olive oil
2 large banana shallots, finely sliced
½ bulb new season garlic, finely chopped
2 chiles de árbol, de-seeded and finely chopped
A small handful of thyme sprigs, leaves picked
Zest of 2 lemons
350ml white wine
500g new potatoes, diced
350g podded or frozen broad beans (a large kilo in their pods)
300g runner beans, top and tailed, cut into 2cm pieces
1 bunch asparagus, woody ends removed, finely sliced on the diagonal, or 300g peas
50–60g Parmesan cheese, to serve

Warm a frying pan over a medium heat and toast the fennel seeds for about 5 minutes to release their flavour before crushing in a pestle and mortar. Cut the fennel bulbs in half lengthways and then cut each half into 3 wedges.

Heat 3 tablespoons of olive oil in a heavy-bottomed saucepan. Add the shallots, garlic, crushed fennel seeds, chilli and thyme. Cook for 5 minutes before adding the fennel and lemon zest. Stir well to coat the fennel in oil, cook for another 5 minutes then turn up the heat and add the white wine. Cook for another 5 minutes, add

the potatoes, broad beans and runner beans, and pour in 700ml water. Bring to the boil and simmer gently for 15 minutes or until some of the liquid has been absorbed and the potatoes are turning tender.

Finally, add the asparagus and the reserved fennel fronds and simmer until the potatoes are cooked through, adding more water if needed. Remove from the heat, season with salt and pepper and a very generous splash of your finest olive oil. Hand round a lump of Parmesan cheese at the table for everyone to grate on.

Serve with garlic-rubbed toast drizzled with olive oil. Don't worry if the vegetables lose their colour, it is the flavour that is important!

Tip – *By all means leave out the asparagus for a more affordable and equally tempting dinner; just make up the weight with other green vegetables.*

Risotto is so therapeutic to make, and this one tastes so good it is like eating in the smartest of restaurants. It is easy to prepare yet smacks of luxury, with the delicate risotto grains swimming in a pool of thick sauce, rich with the flavours of the sea and heady with wine. When I see this on a menu in Spain or Italy I cannot help but order it. Here it is for you to recreate at home, studded with star anise and a light touch of heat from the chilli.

Black risotto with squid ink and gremolata

Feeds 6

60g butter
4 tbsp extra virgin olive oil
2 small onions, finely chopped
2 sticks celery, finely chopped
1 star anise
1½ chile de árbol, crumbled
2 fat garlic cloves, finely chopped
380g arborio or other risotto rice, rinsed in cold water
1.2 litres fish or chicken stock (or even water)
400ml dry white wine
150ml tomato juice
4 sachets squid ink (available from fishmongers and good supermarkets)
450g squid, cleaned and cut into largeish, bite-size pieces

For the gremolata
Grated zest of 1 lemon
Grated zest of 1 orange
A small handful of parsley, finely chopped
1 garlic clove, finely chopped
½ tsp sweet smoked paprika

Heat a heavy-bottomed pan over a medium heat and when hot add two-thirds of the butter and a good slug of olive oil. When the fat begins to sizzle, add the onion, celery, star anise and chilli and season with salt and pepper. Cook the onions for 5–10 minutes, until translucent and soft, before stirring in the garlic.

Cook for another few minutes and then add the rice, stirring to coat all the grains in the fat.

Meanwhile, heat the stock (or water) and white wine together in a separate saucepan and keep warm. Pour the tomato juice and squid ink into the rice and stir well. Now is the time when the risotto needs your undivided attention. Add a small ladle of the hot stock and wine to the risotto and beat it with a wooden spoon, as if you were whipping double cream. When the stock is absorbed, add another ladle and continue to beat off and on until two-thirds of the stock is absorbed. At this point you can turn off the heat, spread the rice out on a tray to cool and finish the recipe later or carry on as below.

Stir all the gremolata ingredients together in a small bowl. Beat the last of the heated stock into the risotto: by this stage the grains will be tender but still with a slight bite in the middle. Cover with greaseproof paper to keep warm for up to 10 minutes.

Heat a large frying pan over your highest flame and when smoking hot add a slug of olive oil. Fry the squid in 2 batches for about a minute a batch until it is just cooked through and golden in places. Stir a knob of butter into the risotto to give it a silky sheen and dish out, topping each plate with a sixth of the squid, a generous sprinkle of the gremolata, a dusting of smoked paprika and a drizzle of extra virgin olive oil.

This is a simple but spectacular dish. I like to bring it to the table and let people help themselves to chunks of succulent fish and the golden potatoes. You can make the paste in advance, and keep the sliced vegetables fresh in a large bowl of cold water. Then just before your friends arrive, put the potatoes in the oven first, followed by the fish as your last guest steps through the front door. They will think you a dab hand.

Brill with potatoes, black olives, orange and fennel

Feeds 6–8

6 anchovies
3 garlic cloves
1 small habanero chilli, de-seeded
2 oranges, zest grated, flesh roughly chopped
A small bunch of thyme or marjoram,
  leaves stripped
120ml extra virgin olive oil
800g waxy potatoes, peeled and sliced into
  ½cm rounds
2 fennel bulbs, trimmed and very finely sliced
1 red onion, very finely sliced
A handful of Kalamata or other black olives,
  de-stoned and roughly chopped
250ml white wine
1.6–1.8kg brill or other flat fish,
  scaled and gutted

Preheat the oven to 220°C/430°F/gas 7.

Put the anchovies, peeled garlic cloves, a few large pinches of salt and the chilli in a pestle and mortar and pound to a paste. Add the zest of the oranges and half the thyme or marjoram and pound some more, slowly adding all but a tablespoon of the olive oil into the paste to combine.

Put the sliced potatoes, fennel, onion, orange flesh and olives in a large mixing bowl and add three-quarters of the anchovy-chilli paste and the rest of the herbs. Toss well together, seasoning with a touch more salt if you think it needs more,

and some black pepper. Arrange across a large baking tray (or 2 trays if you don't have one large enough) and pour over the wine. Place on the top shelf of the oven and roast for 35 minutes.

Season the fish inside and out with salt and black pepper then place on top of the potatoes, drizzle with the remaining oil and paste, scatter with a few more herbs and season.

Roast for a further 25–30 minutes until the fish is just done; you can tell by inserting a skewer. (If there is any resistance the fish needs a little more time but if it goes right in the fish is cooked.) Remove and serve with a crisp green salad.

Tip – *If you are feeding kids you can leave out half the chilli and use fillets of fish instead of whole fish to cut down on bones. Just add the fish to the pan 10 minutes later as the fillets need less cooking time.*

Fried chicken in a light cornflake crumb dusted with paprika and served with a sweet, zingy, jewel-coloured salad. This beautiful summery dish really showcases the tempting array of tomatoes in hues of red, orange, green and yellow that I find at my local market. It's a failsafe recipe that always gets exclamations of pleasure from friends, and better yet, most of the prep can be done a few hours in advance or even the night before.

Chicken schnitzel with fresh tomato and chilli salad

Feeds 4–6

4 chicken breasts, skinless
40g plain flour
1 tsp sweet smoked paprika
100g cornflakes, smashed
40g Parmesan cheese, grated
3 eggs, lightly beaten
30g butter plus a little olive oil

For the tomato salad
6 plum-sized tomatoes (mixed colours, if you can find them), sliced into fat wedges
A good handful of ripe cherry tomatoes (mixed colours, if you can find them), halved or quartered
A handful each of tarragon and mint leaves, roughly chopped
2 limes
4 tbsp good-quality, extra virgin olive oil
1 habanero/Scotch bonnet chilli, de-seeded and finely chopped
½ red onion, sliced very finely
1 tsp caster sugar (optional)

Spread out the chicken breasts on a board and cut them in half horizontally so that you have 2 thinner pieces (or into thirds if you are feeding more people). Mix the flour with the paprika, season generously with salt and pepper and spread out onto a large plate.

Whizz the cornflakes in a food blender, mix with the Parmesan and spread onto another large plate. Beat the eggs in a large bowl. Toss each chicken piece first in the flour, then in the egg and finally in the cornflake mixture. At this stage you can put the chicken pieces in the fridge for a few hours or even overnight, to set the crumbs, or cook straight away.

Make the salad half an hour before you are ready to eat to allow the flavours to ripen at room temperature. Toss the tomatoes gently with the rest of the salad ingredients (perhaps start with half a chilli and see how hot you want to go) including the olive oil and lime juice and season generously with salt and pepper.

Heat a heavy-bottomed frying pan over a medium-high heat and add the fat. Fry the chicken in batches until golden on the outside and cooked through in the middle, about 3–4 minutes for each side. Alternatively, you can fry the chicken briefly in advance and then finish the cooking in a hot oven for 10 minutes just before your friends arrive.

Serve with the salad and piles of mash or boiled new potatoes.

This dish really showcases the tempting array of tomatoes in hues of red, orange, green and yellow.

When I want something healthy and light for lunch I often turn to quinoa. It is such an amazing grain, packed full of protein and other nutrients and incredibly versatile. I particularly like it served warm, though it works at room temperature. This aromatic, summery dish has all the best components of a Coronation salad but uses fish instead of chicken and a light dressing that is heady with all the flavours of its Indian spicing.

Warm Indian quinoa salad with whiting, grapes and almonds

Feeds 4–6

80g almonds, roughly chopped
200g quinoa
400g whiting or other sustainable white fish
1 tbsp vegetable oil
4–5 spring onions, finely chopped
200g white grapes, halved
1 large bunch coriander, chopped
½ lemon

For the dressing
1½ tbsp Garam masala (see page 166)
3 tbsp yoghurt
2 tbsp mayonnaise
1 tsp sugar
1 tbsp white wine vinegar
4 tbsp vegetable oil
2–3cm piece ginger, grated

Toss the almonds in a dry frying pan over a medium heat for 5–10 minutes until they are pale gold and then roughly chop. Cover the quinoa in plenty of water, season well with salt and bring to the boil. Lower the heat and gently simmer for about 20 minutes until the grains release their tadpole-like tails and are tender to the bite. Drain any excess water.

Meanwhile, make the salad dressing by combining the ingredients and mixing well. Toss the warm, drained quinoa in the salad dressing.

Put the grill on its highest setting, season the fish with salt and pepper and a trickle of oil and grill, skin side down, for about 5 minutes or until the flesh has turned opaque through the fillet. Flake the flesh into largeish pieces, discarding the skin.

Toss the almonds, spring onions, grapes and coriander into the dressed quinoa, then stir in the flakes of fish. Squeeze over the half lemon, check the seasoning and serve at once.

Heady with all the flavours
4 its Indian Spicing.

We were in Thailand, enjoying a break from the beating sun at a local restaurant by the sea, when I tried a delicious plate of what seemed to be crumbs of deep-fried fish with coconut and red curry paste. I came back to London determined to recreate the dish, tried several times unsuccessfully, and in the process happily came up with this recipe. It is perfection with the Coconut rice on page 187.

Thai red curry coconut prawns

Feeds 4

3 tbsp palm sugar
2 tbsp fish sauce
3 tbsp coconut milk
2 tbsp Thai red curry paste (see page 21)
Zest of 2 limes, juice of 1
½ tsp chilli flakes
300g (MSC certified) king prawns, de-veined
5 tbsp vegetable oil
2 banana shallots, finely sliced
3 garlic cloves, finely sliced
1 bunch coriander, leaves roughly chopped
1 lime, cut into wedges

Melt the sugar in a small pan over a gentle heat. Add the fish sauce, coconut milk and red curry paste and stir for a few minutes over the heat until the sauce looks thick and smooth and smells good. Remove from the heat and add the lime zest and the juice of one lime, plus the chilli flakes. Check for seasoning, adding a little more fish sauce if you like or a pinch of salt. Leave to cool and then pour over the prawns and marinate for at least an hour.

Heat the oil in a large wok over a medium-high heat and add the shallots. Stir-fry until crisp and a light caramel colour, stirring fairly frequently so as not to burn them. Remove with a slotted spoon to a plate covered with kitchen paper. Repeat with the garlic, turning the heat up a little and frying until light gold. If you burn either they will taste bitter.

Now drain away all but a tablespoon of the oil and turn the heat right up. When it is sizzling hot scoop the prawns from the marinade and stir-fry for a few minutes until golden and cooked through (they will turn from translucent to an opaque pink colour; try not to overcook or they will be tough). Now add the rest of the marinade and stir to heat through for a minute.

Serve over the Coconut rice (page 187), scattered with the shallots, garlic and chopped coriander and garnished with wedges of lime.

Photo on the following page.

Sometimes one has to shrug one's shoulders and accept that certain things in life are expensive; fillet steak is one. I adore cheaper cuts like skirt and rib-eye for their character, but in certain recipes only the fillet will do. This dish is a real treat so save it for when you want to spoil yourself and your guests. The aromatic spice rub brings out the flavour of the beef whilst searing the joint gives it a masculine edge that contrasts beautifully with the buttery, soft texture within.

Thai style grilled beef
with a quinoa and cherry tomato salad

Feeds 4–6

A 500g piece of fillet beef
150g green beans, topped, tailed and halved
100g quinoa
2 tsp balsamic vinegar
Juice of 1 lime
3 tbsp olive oil
250g cherry tomatoes, quartered
3 spring onions, trimmed and finely sliced
1 bunch mint, leaves picked, large leaves torn
1 bunch coriander, leaves roughly chopped
Dipping sauce (see page 164)

For the marinade
½ tsp dried chilli flakes or roast chilli powder
  (see page 15)
3 garlic cloves, peeled
1 tsp peppercorns
2 tbsp coriander seeds
1–2 tbsp finely chopped coriander root (or
  stalks)
2 tbsp demerara sugar
2 tbsp soy sauce

For the marinade, put the chilli, garlic, peppercorns and coriander seeds in a pestle and mortar with a good few pinches of salt and bash to a paste. Work in the chopped coriander root and the demerara sugar and finally stir in the soy sauce. Rub this marinade all over the beef fillet and refrigerate for several hours or overnight. Cook the green beans in simmering water for about 5–6 minutes until tender but still with

a little bite. Cover the quinoa in double its volume of water, season with salt and cook until the grains release their tadpole-like tails and are tender to the bite. Drain any excess water, then toss the warm quinoa with the balsamic vinegar, lime juice and olive oil. Add the beans, tomatoes, spring onions and herbs.

Take the beef fillet out of the fridge about half an hour before you are ready to eat and allow it to come to room temperature. Heat a chargrill over your highest flame for a good 10 minutes and meanwhile remove the beef from the marinade, pat dry and rub with a few drops of oil.

When the chargrill is smoking hot sear the beef for about a minute on all sides so that its surface is charred but the centre is still very rare, about 4–5 minutes in total. Allow the beef to rest for 10 minutes before cutting into wafer thin slices. Serve slices of the beef fanned out onto large plates, dressed with the dipping sauce, the quinoa on the side and, if you like, some boiled, buttered potatoes.

Tip – *Fillet is seriously expensive, so when the coffers are low you could serve this recipe as a starter instead, halving the amount of beef and the cost. Follow with a simple main course like risotto or a delicious pasta dish.*

Turn over for a photo.

I watched the Masterchef finalist Alex Rushmar cook a version of this in his restaurant in Cambridge and it screamed out at me. The sticky, complex-tasting sauce is sensationally good and pretty easy to make. You can marinate the meat and make the sauce ahead of time and the result is an unusual, citrus-sharp sauce that manages to straddle the boundaries between sweet and savoury. It is also great with ham.

Duck breast with caramel seven-spice sauce

Feeds 4–6

2 duck breasts (600–700g meat)
4 tsp seven-spice powder (see page 166)
200g unrefined caster sugar
Zest and juice of 2 lemons
Zest and juice of 1 orange
5 tbsp port
300ml stock
1 tbsp butter

Use a sharp knife to score the duck skin in a criss-cross pattern. Rub the breasts all over with 2 teaspoons of the seven-spice powder, then leave to marinate in the fridge for at least a few hours.

To make the caramel, put the remaining seven-spice powder, citrus zest and juices, port and 100ml stock in a jug. Add the rest of the stock and the sugar to a saucepan over a high heat. Continue to heat the sugar until it is starting to darken in patches, swirling the pan to mix the caramel. When it has turned a deep brown all over pour in the contents of the jug, taking care as the sauce will bubble up and splutter. Turn the heat down and stir until the sugar has melted again then simmer briskly for about 10–15 minutes until you have a glossy sauce. Pour through a fine sieve for a velvety finish. Taste and adjust the seasoning with salt and pepper if you think it needs it.

Take the duck breasts out of the fridge about half an hour before you are ready to eat and allow them to come to room temperature. Preheat the oven to 180°C/350°F/gas 4.

Heat a frying pan over a medium heat and when the pan is hot add the butter, swirl it around and then add the duck breasts skin side down. Cook the duck for 5 minutes until the skin is golden and crisp, pouring out any fat it releases as you cook (you can save it for roast potatoes). Briefly turn the breasts over and sear on the other side for 1 minute before transferring to the oven and cooking for 5 more minutes. Allow to rest somewhere warm for 10 minutes.

Cut the breasts into thin slices and serve with the warm sauce. I recently cooked this with a tray of roast Jerusalem artichokes and a fennel and pomegranate salad and it went down a treat. It would also be delicious with Sweet potato mash (page 185) or even some plain boiled new potatoes or rice.

Tip – *If you are prone to panicking about whether the meat is cooked, worry not. Stick in a skewer after 10 minutes of resting and if the juices are bloody you can always pop it back in the oven for a few more minutes until cooked to your liking – people never mind having extra drinking time!*

I love the French classic of rabbit cooked in tarragon and mustard, but marjoram is often easier to find, which is how I came up with this bastardised version. The chilli adds another dimension, giving a light seasoning of heat to the silky combination of cream, Dijon mustard, sweet shallots and caramelised meat. When the pot comes out of the oven and the lid is lifted, all those flavours, which have been slowly simmering together, release an incredible smell into the kitchen.

Pot roast rabbit
with oregano and mustard

Feeds 4–6

**A handful of marjoram leaves,
  roughly chopped**
5 tbsp Dijon mustard
**2 rabbits (bought from a good butcher),
  jointed**
Plain flour, to dust
50g butter
A dash of olive oil
14 baby shallots, peeled and halved
200g streaky bacon, chopped
**2 small chiles de árbol, de-seeded
  and crumbled**
3 fat garlic cloves, crushed
250ml white wine
300ml double cream

Preheat the oven to 140°C/275°F/gas 1.
Mix the marjoram and mustard together and smear all over the rabbit joints. Season well with salt and pepper, then lightly coat the rabbit pieces in flour.

Melt a third of the butter in a large casserole dish over a medium heat and when it is sizzling hot, briefly brown the pieces on all sides. Remove them to a plate. Add the rest of the butter to the pan along with a slug of olive oil and the shallots, fry for a few minutes then add the bacon and chilli. After a few more minutes put in the garlic and cook until the bacon and shallots are coloured but not burnt. Pour in the wine so that it bubbles up and then the cream. Return the rabbit pieces to the dish and bring everything up to a very gentle simmer. Cover with a lid and cook in the oven for about an hour or until just tender. Wild rabbit will take a little longer.

Serve with the mash on page 185 and a fresh green salad.

Tip – *I like to use farmed rabbit for this recipe, as I prefer its tender flavour, but wild rabbit will provide a richer and gamier taste and is totally free-range. If you do use the latter, salted water will help tenderise the meat – simply dissolve a couple of tablespoons of salt into hot water and then add enough cold water to completely submerge the rabbit. Put it in the fridge and after a few hours take it out and pat the meat dry.*

In China, pork belly is often the most expensive cut as the fat in it is much prized for its succulent flavour. In this recipe it is braised soft, and then roasted to crisp a little. The soft yielding flesh is deliciously spiced with Asian aromatics. This is delicious served with nutty brown rice or Sweet potato mash (see page 185) and some sautéed greens. Best of all it can be made ahead and heated up in the oven just before you want to eat.

Asian slow-cooked pork belly

Feeds 6–8

2 heads of garlic
1 pork belly (about 2.2kg)
200ml dry sherry (Manzanilla is best, or fino)
200ml soy sauce
3 tbsp soft brown sugar
3 star anise
1 long cinnamon stick
2 chipotle chillies, de-stemmed
50ml saba or good-quality balsamic vinegar
15 thin slices of ginger

To serve
2 tbsp cornflour
2 fresh red chillies, de-seeded and finely sliced
A large handful of coriander, roughly chopped, roots and stems removed
A small bunch of spring onions, finely sliced on the bias

Separate out the garlic cloves by smashing the heads with a rolling pin a few times, then smash each clove to release the skin easily.

Put the pork in a large pan and cover with water (if you need to, cut the joint in half). Bring to the boil, turn down the heat and simmer very gently, scooping off any scum with a slotted spoon.

Preheat the oven to 130°C/250°F/gas ½. When the pork has simmered for 30 minutes, pour out half of the cooking water and add the rest of the braising ingredients, and the coriander roots and stems. Bring to the boil and cook in the oven for about 2 hours until the meat offers no resistance when a skewer is inserted.

Remove the pork from its braising liquid and pull out the rib bones from the meat. At this stage you can cool the pork ready to heat up just before you eat.

Mix a few tablespoons of cold water into the cornflour to make a paste and stir into the pork braising liquid. Simmer briskly for 15–20 minutes until it is reduced to a glossy sauce.

Preheat the oven to its highest setting about 40 minutes before you are ready to eat. When the oven is hot, baste the pork in a few tablespoons of the sauce and roast for 20 minutes in the oven. Serve thin slices of the pork scattered with the red chilli, coriander and spring onions and spoonfuls of the rich, aromatic sauce.

Or try... *The leftovers make a gloriously quick supper. Chill any leftover pork overnight. Slice it thinly across the layers of fat and meat. Heat a tablespoon of oil in a wok and stir-fry with a crumbled chile de árbol for a few minutes until lightly browned. Add a few tablespoons of chilli bean paste, fry for a few minutes, then add fine slices of 3 washed leeks, or broccoli. Stir-fry before adding the rest of the cooking stock from the night before.*

Being a novice to Asian food I thought I'd hit the jackpot when I first tried this hot and sour minced pork salad in a little restaurant outside Angkor Wat, Cambodia. It was savoury and mouth-wateringly good, the perfect illustration of how umami can hit you with its terrific flavour. A few months later we had dinner with a friend, Lexi; she made a laab with chicken not pork and served it like this. It makes great party food so save it for when you go a bit mad and ask 12 for supper (just treble the recipe).

Addictive pork laab salad

Feeds 4

70g long-grain white rice
1 tsp vegetable oil
500g minced pork
300ml chicken stock
3 Kaffir lime leaves
4 fat sticks lemongrass, finely chopped
2 tsp Roast chilli powder (see page 162)
  or 1 tsp Turkish chilli flakes
1 tsp caster sugar
3 banana shallots, very finely sliced
Juice of 2–3 limes
6 tbsp fish sauce
A large bunch of coriander, roots and leaves
  separated, roots chopped
A large bunch of mint, leaves picked
1 large iceberg lettuce or 1 Chinese leaf
  cabbage, leaves separated
A couple of crushed dried chillies, to serve
A bowl of hoisin sauce, to serve

Heat a small, heavy-bottomed pan and dry-toast the raw rice for a few minutes, stirring as you do until it starts turning pale golden and smelling deliciously nutty and biscuity. Grind in a pestle and mortar or spice grinder to a fine powder.

Heat the oil in a wok over a medium-high heat and add the pork. Stir-fry for a few minutes, breaking it up with a spoon before adding the stock, lime leaves, lemongrass, chilli, sugar and half the shallots. Simmer over a very gentle heat for 10 minutes, breaking up the pork into tiny crumbs.

Add the juice of 2 limes, the fish sauce and the roast rice and stir to combine. Cook for a minute or two before tasting. I like to season with a good pinch of salt but it may also need a little more lime juice or fish sauce – adjust the seasoning to your palate. Stir in the rest of the shallots and the coriander roots.

Serve the pork in the middle of the table in a pretty bowl with bowls of picked mint and coriander leaves, lettuce, chillies and sauce. Encourage everyone to help themselves to lettuce leaves to make a pork wrap with all the trimmings.

Tip – *This is delicious served with a bowl of Coconut rice (see page 187).*

Lamb is always such a treat and although I love lamb chops or a leg still pink and juicy in the middle, there is something irresistible about a shoulder cooked long and slow until it is falling apart and melting in its own juices. This voluptuous dish is made for the weekend, when all you want to do is throw a joint in the oven and not worry too much about the timings. The rich flavour of lamb lends itself perfectly to exotic, warm Middle Eastern spices.

Middle Eastern rose-scented, falling apart lamb

Feeds 6–8

1 shoulder of lamb (about 2kg)
2 heads of garlic
2 tsp cumin seeds
2.5cm cinnamon stick
1 tbsp coriander seeds
1 tbsp sea salt
3 tbsp Harissa (see page 167)
1 lemon, zested and quartered
2 tbsp extra virgin olive oil
1 tbsp rose syrup (optional)
1 kg acorn squash, peeled and cut into
  (roughly) 2cm chunks
500ml dry white wine

Trim the shoulder of lamb of its outside layer of fat and make incisions all over the flesh. The fat is normally dry and comes away easily with a knife. Cut the heads of garlic in half and slip the cloves from one of the halves out of their skins into a pestle and mortar, leaving the remaining 3 halves for later. Heat the spices in a dry frying pan for a minute or two to bring out their flavour and then add to the pestle and mortar with the salt. Grind to a rough paste before adding the harissa, lemon zest, olive oil and rose syrup, if using.

Rub the lamb shoulder with the spice paste and leave to marinate for at least a few hours, preferably overnight.

Four hours before you are ready to eat, preheat the oven to 190°C/375°F/gas 5. Lay the squash out on a deep baking tray with the lemon quarters and the rest of the garlic and place the lamb on top. Roast for half an hour, then turn the heat down to 130°C/250°F/gas ½, add the wine and continue to cook the lamb for another 3½ hours or until the meat is falling away from the bone and smells enticing.

Serve with the pilau rice on page 90, omitting the carrots, and the coriander raita on page 172.

Throw a joint in the oven and don't worry too much about the timings.

6

weekend
treats

Weekends are the high point of any week, a time of excruciating excitement that begins to build on Thursday morning and by Friday night is threatening to explode (I do keep thinking I will grow out of my love of weekends, but so far I haven't). Weekends are when we're all together, working out how we're going to spend the next few days, trying to pack in as much fun as possible around the inevitable few, humdrum chores.

This is the time that we can see friends or revel in our own company – time for slow, lazy starts to the day with sweetcorn fritters and chilli-spiked French toast whilst we deliberate on our plans for the precious few days ahead. If we have friends over it is more fun to cook something where the girls will be able to join in (my youngest, Twiglet, may be only six months old, but I have high hopes).

My husband is an expert in baking so he would be in charge of the dough for the Chorizo, new potato and chile de árbol pizza (and my two-year-old, Tati, would get herself covered in it). I, being the chilli fiend, would be the one to make a slow-cooked shin of beef studded with the deep earthy tones of pasilla chilli and sweet, caramelised onions, making it perhaps late Saturday afternoon to feast upon on Sunday. At lunch we might assemble the beautifully kid-friendly but potentially fiery Lebanese-inspired lamb wraps or our ultimate club sandwich – both of which make the business of fuelling a family infinitely more fun than just plonking out bread and cheese on the table.

If a few friends decided to turn up for an impromptu dinner on Saturday night I would roll out a few tried-and-tested winners: the wonderfully hot and spicy Grilled Malaysian-style chicken or the warm, comforting Spinach pastilla pie. Weekends were built for fun and food can become part of that fun. Roll on Friday!

Waffles used to be a great tradition when we went to stay with my grandmother in Wales. She was from Tennessee and had a proper old-fashioned, cast iron waffle iron; breakfasts were always a huge treat there. Hurrying to feed a room full of hungry people the other day, I decided to experiment with the classic pairing of maple syrup and bacon but with the much easier-to-make French toast. The result was a room full of very happy people!

Orange-spiced French toast with bacon and maple syrup

Feeds 4–6

3 large eggs
100ml whole milk
5 tbsp maple syrup, plus extra for
  drizzling on top
A few good pinches of cayenne pepper
1 tsp vanilla extract
Zest and juice of ½ orange
30g butter
6–8 thick slices of brioche
12–16 rashers of streaky bacon

Whisk the eggs briefly and then whisk in the milk, 5 tablespoons of maple syrup, the cayenne, vanilla extract and orange. If you like, season with a small pinch of salt.

Heat a frying pan over a high heat, add a tiny knob of butter, swirl it around to coat the whole pan and fry the bacon in 2 batches until crisp. Keep warm.

Melt a little more butter in the pan over a medium heat. Dip the brioche slices in the egg mixture, shake to get rid of any excess and fry the slices, a few at a time, until golden on both sides.

Serve the brioche with the bacon and more maple syrup to pour on top.

These were adapted from a Nigel Slater recipe but, because of my love for all things Spanish, I have given them a more Latin feel with smoked paprika, one of my favourite store cupboard ingredients. This is a lovely easy dish that requires very little work.

Stuffed peppers with pork, smoked paprika and thyme

Feeds 4–6

6 tbsp extra virgin olive oil
1 onion, finely diced
1 fennel bulb, trimmed and diced
400g minced pork
2 garlic cloves, crushed
6–8 sprigs of thyme, leaves stripped from branches
1 tsp fennel seeds, crushed
1 tsp sweet smoked paprika
1 x 400g tin plum tomatoes
A glass of white wine or sherry (optional)
3 large red peppers, halved and cored
A large handful of breadcrumbs
A good pinch of chilli flakes
30–40g Parmesan cheese, for grating

Preheat the oven to 190°C/375°F/gas 5.

Heat half the oil in a heavy-bottomed saucepan, then add the onion and fennel and sweat over a medium heat for 5 minutes. Turn the heat up and add half the pork, the garlic, thyme, fennel seeds and paprika and fry the ingredients, breaking up the pork with a wooden spoon as you go. When the pork is broken up into the size of small crumbs, add another 2 tablespoons of olive oil and the rest of the meat and repeat the process, then season generously with salt and pepper.

Stir in the tomatoes and, if you have a bottle open, a glass of good white wine (or sherry), then simmer for 5 minutes to reduce the liquid to a sauce.

Season the peppers with a little salt and pepper and stuff with the pork mixture. Bake in the oven for 15 minutes before sprinkling the peppers with the breadcrumbs, chilli flakes and Parmesan and drizzling with the rest of the olive oil. Cook for another 25–30 minutes until the peppers are soft and the breadcrumbs have turned a golden brown. Serve with a bowl of rice and, if you like, a green salad.

Tip – *You can substitute the pork for steamed, diced potatoes for a great vegetarian supper.*

If ever there was a cunning way to get children to eat their greens, this is it. Okay, so it is probably cheating (Tati, my eldest, would eat almost anything if it had a few raisins thrown in), but it is nonetheless a delicious meat-free pie that you can make as a glamourous side dish for a dinner party or a very luxurious-tasting weekend supper. Even my husband joins the fray when fighting for the last piece. The cayenne lends a very mild bite to the dish, but alter it according to taste.

Spinach pastilla pie

Feeds 4–6

You will need a frying pan with an ovenproof handle or a shallow, round baking dish, 23–25cm diameter

90g currants
A splash of rum (optional)
3 tbsp pine nuts
500g spinach, washed, large stalks removed
3 tbsp olive oil
1 small red onion, peeled and finely chopped
1 garlic clove, crushed
½ tsp cayenne pepper, plus a little for dusting
100g Parmesan cheese, freshly grated
75g feta, crumbled
2 eggs, lightly beaten
Zest of 1 lemon
70g melted butter
4 sheets filo pastry
A pinch of icing sugar, for dusting

Preheat the oven to 180°C/350°F/gas 4. Cover the currants with boiling water and if you have a little rum add a splash. Bake the pine nuts in the oven until golden brown.

Cook the spinach in a large pan over a medium heat, sprinkle with 3 tablespoons of water and season generously with salt and pepper. Once it's wilted, squeeze the spinach through a sieve to get rid of excess water, then roughly chop.

Heat the olive oil in a heavy-bottomed pan, then add the onion and cook for 5–10 minutes, until translucent and soft. Stir in the garlic, then season with salt and cayenne pepper. Add the drained spinach to the pan and heat through. Drain the currants and add to the spinach along with the pine nuts. Add the Parmesan, feta, eggs and lemon zest and allow to cool.

Grease the ovenproof pan with melted butter. Lay 3 sheets of filo pastry in the tin at angles, brushing them with butter as you go, making sure that some of the sheets hang over the sides of the pan. You want a pastry overhang of about 8–10cm so that you can fold it back over the filling to bake in the oven. Now fill the pastry with the spinach mixture.

Place the last piece of filo on top of the filling and fold in the overhanging pastry. Brush again with the melted butter and bake for 15–20 minutes or until the pastry is golden. If you like, transfer to the hob and heat for a few minutes to ensure that the bottom is crisp.

Slide the pie out onto a large plate and dust lightly with cayenne pepper and a little icing sugar. This makes a very good dinner with a mixed leaf salad.

Tip – *If you want less of a bite use sweet smoked paprika or Turkish chilli flakes in the recipe instead of the cayenne.*

These are perfect Sunday brunch material. We always have frozen corn in the freezer and invariably there is chorizo in the fridge or freezer as it is such a brilliantly handy ingredient to have in the house. These fritters are quick to prepare and take even less time to cook. If you like, pop a tray of cherry tomatoes in a low oven at the start and they will be roasted to perfection just as the fritters are ready to eat.

Sweetcorn and chorizo fritters

Feeds 4–6

60g butter
150g chorizo, diced into 1cm cubes
180g plain flour
1 tsp baking powder
A pinch of sugar
450g fresh or frozen sweetcorn kernels
  (4 corn on the cobs)
2 eggs and 1 egg yolk
100ml full-fat milk
1–2 tsp chipotles en adobo (see page 169),
  depending on how spicy you like 'em!
3 spring onions, finely sliced
A small handful of fresh coriander,
  roughly chopped

Heat a third of the butter in a hot frying pan and add the chorizo. Fry until the chorizo has released some of its red, delicious fat and is cooked through.

Meanwhile, sift the flour, baking powder and sugar into a large mixing bowl. In another bowl whisk half the corn with the eggs, half the milk and the cooked chipotle. Make a well in the centre of the flour, whisk in the egg mix then gradually add the rest of the milk until you get the mixture about as thick as double cream, so that it drops off the spoon in thickish dollops.

Melt the rest of the butter and add half of it to the batter before folding in the rest of the corn, the spring onions, chorizo and chopped coriander. Season to taste with salt and pepper.

To fry the pancakes, heat a heavy-bottomed, non-stick pan until it is smoking hot and then brush with a little of the remaining melted butter. Dollop out a couple of large dessert spoons of the mixture, spaced well apart so that the fritters don't run into each other (or make them one at a time if your pan is small). Fry over a medium heat for about 2 minutes a side until golden brown. You need to adjust the heat of the pan so that the fritters cook all the way through without burning.

The fritters will last a few days wrapped in the fridge. Just reheat them in the oven or frying pan.

Tip – *These are also great with a fried egg and some fresh salsa or with avocado cream. Whizz a few avocados in a food blender with the juice of 1 lime, some fresh basil, 2 tablespoons of crème fraiche and a touch of olive oil. If you like, add half a de-seeded, chopped fresh green chilli. This is also delicious with the Tomato, ginger and chilli jam on page 179 and a good dollop of crème fraiche.*

If you are a fan of tuna you'll love this sandwich, filled with tangy mayonnaise-style sauce blitzed with anchovies and capers. In Italy they serve it with veal but I find it makes the perfect partner for eggs and cress. A good shaking of hot sauce cuts through its richness and heightens the flavours. This is a great weekend lunch when you have friends coming over and want something enticing but not too fancy. As with all things chilli-related, add as much hot sauce as you like.

Tonnata with egg and cress

Feeds 4

4 eggs (at room temperature)
2 handfuls of watercress
4 granary baps or 8 slices of bread (optional)
Everyday hot sauce (page 176), Wahaca's chile
  de árbol sauce or Tabasco, to serve

For the mayo
2 egg yolks
1 fat garlic clove
1 tsp Dijon mustard
2 tbsp capers, rinsed and drained
150ml olive oil
1 x 160g tin (line-caught Skipjack)
  tuna in olive oil
4 anchovies
1 tbsp white wine vinegar
A good squeeze of lemon juice

Lower the eggs into a small saucepan of boiling water and cook at a gentle simmer for 7 minutes. Drain, then plunge into ice cold water until completely cool (about 10 minutes).

To make the mayo, put the yolks, garlic, mustard and capers into the clean bowl of a food mixer and season generously with pepper and a good pinch of salt. Whizz to a purée and then, with the machine running, slowly drizzle in the oil drop by drop to start and then slowly and steadily in a thin stream until you have a lovely thick sauce. Now add the tuna, still whizzing, followed by the anchovies, vinegar and lemon juice.

Crack the now cool eggs all over with lots of little taps (which will make peeling easy) and peel. Cut the eggs into quarters and put them on a board with a bowl of the tuna sauce, a pile of watercress and some fresh bread, and a bottle of hot sauce. A bowl of cherry tomatoes would be fun too. Or simply pack the mayo into sandwiches with the watercress, slices of the egg and a generous shake of hot sauce. The leftover mayo makes a great salad dressing thinned down with a little vinaigrette.

Add as much hot sauce as you like

I have always been a sucker for a good sandwich. I first tried a club on a year abroad in Chile, feeling very scruffy and out of place at a smart country club. Biting into the familiar-tasting upmarket version of a BLT was intensely comforting. Those powerful associations have stayed firmly in my memory ever since. I came up with this version when I had some chipotle mayo left over and was feeling in need of something restorative.

The ultimate chicken club sandwich

Feeds 4

A small handful of thyme leaves, chopped
2 bay leaves, crumbled or finely chopped
2 garlic cloves, crushed
2–3 tbsp olive oil
4 chicken thighs
10 rashers of smoked streaky bacon
5–6 heaped tbsp Chipotle mayonnaise
  (see page 170)
4 large ciabatta rolls, sliced in half
25g butter (at room temperature), for
  spreading
1–2 tbsp grainy mustard
2 beef tomatoes, cut into 1cm slices
2 Granny Smith apples, cut into wafer-thin
  slices across the core
2 baby gems, leaves separated

The sharp sweetness of the Granny Smith is a perfect contrast to the smoky mayo and salty bacon

Place the herbs, garlic, bay and oil in a pestle & mortar and pound together. Add the chicken, mixing well. Leave for at least 30 minutes.

Preheat the oven to 200°C/390°F/gas 6 and preheat the grill to its highest setting. Heat a chargrill over your highest flame and put the chicken pieces skin side down on the grill. Cook for 5 minutes until the skin is browned and crisp before turning and briefly browning on the other side. Transfer to a baking tray and roast in the oven for 25–30 minutes, until the juices run clear when you stick a skewer into them. Remove from the oven and set aside.

Meanwhile, grill the bacon until the edges are crisp and caramelised. When the chicken has cooled, tear off the bone and into smallish pieces and toss in the mayonnaise. Toast the ciabatta, butter the top half liberally and spread with a little mustard. Pile the chicken mayo onto the bottom half and top with tomato slices, 3–4 slices of apple, a few rashers of bacon and a few leaves of baby gem. Somehow manage to put the top on and press down firmly to compact the sandwich. Either secure with a toothpick, which you can decorate with sparkly stickers (always fun), or cut the sandwiches in half for easier eating. Eat with or without a side order of crisps!

Tip – *If you don't have a chargrill just place the chicken straight into the oven and roast for 5 minutes longer. This is great with extra hot sauce on the side, or the chilli oil on page 163.*

Malay cooking is a mouth-watering melting pot of tastes from China, India and other parts of Asia, which I have only recently discovered. If you've made last-minute plans to see a bunch of friends at the weekend and wonder what you're going to give them, look no further. This recipe is simple to prepare and enticingly hot and savoury, with the final grill rendering the chicken skin irresistible.

Grilled Malaysian-style chicken

Feeds 6

1 tsp cumin seeds
1 cinnamon stick
2 chiles de árbol or Kashmiri chillies
20g macadamia nuts
1 onion, peeled and quartered
4 garlic cloves, peeled
2 large fresh chillies plus 2 bird's eye chillies, de-stemmed
5cm piece of galangal or ginger, peeled and finely sliced
4 lime leaves
3 tbsp vegetable oil
1.2kg chicken thighs and drumsticks, skin on and bone in
1 x 400ml tin coconut milk

Toast the cumin, cinnamon and dry chillies in a dry frying pan for a few minutes over a medium heat, shaking fairly continuously until they start smelling fragrant. Grind them to a powder in a pestle and mortar or spice grinder with the macadamia nuts. Add them to a food processor with the rest of the ingredients apart from the chicken and coconut milk and whizz to a smoothish paste.

Cover the chicken with the paste and heat a wok over a medium high heat. Add the chicken pieces and stir-fry for about 10-15 minutes until the skin has turned a lovely golden brown. Pour in the coconut milk, stir thoroughly and cook for another 10 minutes, stirring occasionally until the pieces are cooked through. All this can be done in advance and at this stage the chicken can be cooled and refrigerated.

When you are ready to eat turn on the grill to medium-high and grill the chicken pieces, skin side up, until golden, blistered and crisp (if you are re-heating make sure the chicken is heated through). Serve the chicken with greens and rice, preferably the coconut rice on page 187.

This simple recipe was inspired by the flat-style pizzas they sell after hours on the streets of Oaxaca. The base is delicious and incredibly satisfying to make (or you can buy ready-made pizza dough mixes in the shops). The combination of creamy mozzarella and avocado provides a wonderful foil for the highly spiced chorizo and fiery chilli oil; a scattering of peppery rocket adds the finishing touch to a complex-tasting, gutsy pizza that you will want to make over and over again.

Chorizo, new potato and chile de árbol pizza

Feeds 4–6 (makes 3 x 30cm pizzas)

500g new potatoes, scrubbed
Olive oil
500g mozzarella (or 2 large balls)
120g thinly sliced chorizo
A small bunch of thyme, leaves picked
80g Parmesan cheese, freshly grated
Chilli oil (see page 163), to drizzle
2 handfuls of rocket
1–2 avocados, peeled, de-stoned and sliced

For the pizza dough
5g dried yeast
275ml warm water
400g type '00' or strong bread flour,
  plus more for rolling
1–2 tsp fine sea salt
A good slug of extra virgin olive oil
A good pinch of sugar

For the dough, mix the yeast, sugar and olive oil with the water and leave to sit for a few minutes.

Sift the flour into a large bowl (or the bowl of a food mixer) and make a well in the middle. Pour in the yeast mix and using a fork, gradually bring in the flour from the sides and swirl it into the liquid to form a wet dough. Then knead by hand, or with a dough hook, until the dough is satiny and smooth. Put it in a clean bowl, cover with a damp cloth and leave in a warm room for 90 minutes or until the dough has doubled in size.

Meanwhile, preheat the oven to 240°C/465°F/ gas 9, or to its highest setting, and place a baking stone inside. Alternatively, use a baking tray lined with non-stick paper or dusted with flour. Simmer the potatoes until just tender in boiling, salted water. Cool slightly and then slice into thin rounds.

Flour your hands and the worktop, then punch down the dough, knead for a few minutes and divide into three. Shape each piece into a ball and roll out on a lightly floured surface into 5mm thick rounds or, if you prefer, long, round oblongs. You can roll these out 20 minutes before baking. Transfer to a couple of well-floured baking sheets.

Drizzle the dough with a little olive oil, then top with torn up little pieces of the mozzarella, the potato slices, chorizo, thyme and Parmesan and some chile de árbol oil. Slide the first pizza onto the hot stone or baking sheet and bake for 15 minutes, or until crispy and golden. Scatter with rocket, more chile de árbol oil, sea salt and slices of avocado. Eat up!

This recipe lies somewhere between the watermelon and feta salad that Peter Gordon featured in his Sugar Club Cookbook *in the 1990s, and a Middle Eastern fattoush, or chopped salad. I adore the way the crisp, baked pitta pieces lap up the salad dressing in a fattoush, but find all that crunchy veg a touch overwhelming. This is just as flavourful, but suits a gentler, less robust mood. Some ideas of what to serve it with are photographed on the next page!*

Feta, watermelon and pitta crisp salad

Feeds 4

**3 pieces of pitta bread
  (preferably wholemeal)**
2 tbsp olive oil
1 tsp hot smoked paprika
½ small watermelon
½ cauliflower
200g feta, crumbled
1 small red onion
1 tsp cumin seeds, toasted
1 small garlic clove
1 tsp Dijon mustard
2 tbsp red wine vinegar
**6 tbsp extra virgin olive oil plus
  extra for drizzling**
**A small handful each of parsley and
  mint leaves, roughly chopped**

Preheat the oven to 180°C/350°F/gas 4.

Use a sharp knife to butterfly open the pitta breads and place the halves face-up on a baking sheet. Drizzle over a couple of tablespoons of olive oil, sprinkle with the smoked paprika and a pinch of sea salt and bake in the oven for 5–10 minutes, until the pittas are crisp and golden.

Meanwhile, cut the watermelon into quarters lengthways, and then cut each quarter in half: the smaller the wedges, the easier the peeling. Cut away the flesh from the thick rind and cut the flesh into rough cubes about 2cm across. I don't bother taking out the seeds as I find them easy enough to swallow or fish out when eating.

Slice the cauliflower into fine shards – it will break up and fall apart as you slice but don't worry about that. You're after thin, slender whispers of cauliflower rather than large thick pieces. Peel, halve and finely slice the red onion.

Crush the cumin seeds and the garlic in a pestle and mortar with a good pinch of sea salt. Add the mustard and vinegar, mash, then stir in the olive oil.

Break the pitta bread into chunks into a salad bowl and toss with the remaining ingredients and the salad dressing. Serve at once.

This came about after a long day at work, daydreaming of an old recipe I used to cook, a pizza topped with a kick-ass seasoned, minced lamb. I stopped at a butcher's to buy the meat, but of course by the time I arrived home it was late and I was bushed. This was the result: a really fun weekend dinner, full of fresh ingredients, bright herbs and rich Middle Eastern flavours. I love the lamb wrapped in pitta, but you can just as easily serve it with rice. See the photo overleaf.

Lebanese lamb wraps

Feeds 4

600g minced lamb
3 tbsp extra virgin olive oil
1 large onion, finely chopped
2 tsp ground cumin
2 tsp ground cinnamom
3 garlic cloves
½ tsp Turkish chilli flakes or cayenne pepper
  (optional)
2 tbsp pomegranate molasses
6 large wholemeal pittas

For the garlicky yoghurt
125g yoghurt
1 tbsp tahini
1 garlic clove, crushed
Juice of ½ lemon

For the salad
300g cherry tomatoes
A large bunch of flat leaf parsley, roughly
  chopped
½ red onion, very finely sliced
Juice of ½ lemon
1–2 tbsp pomegranate molasses
3 tbsp extra virgin olive oil
A few good pinches of sugar, to taste
1 fresh red chilli, finely chopped (de-seed if you
  want it less spicy)

Season the lamb with salt and pepper. Put a wide, heavy-bottomed pan over a high heat, add a tablespoon of olive oil and half the lamb. Stir-fry for 3–4 minutes, breaking up the meat with a wooden spoon, until the meat is browned, then set aside and repeat with the rest of the mince. De-glaze the pan with a few tablespoons of water and pour into the cooked mince. Add another few tablespoons of oil to the pan, turn the heat down to medium and add the onion and spices, frying for 5–10 minutes until the onion is soft and translucent but not coloured. Add the garlic cloves and the chilli (if using), season generously with salt and pepper and cook for another minute before adding 2 tablespoons of pomegranate molasses and 200ml water. Simmer for 5 minutes to bring the flavours together, then check for seasoning.

Meanwhile, mix the yoghurt with the tahini, garlic and lemon juice. Season to taste.

Toss the salad ingredients together. Warm the pitta through and put on the table with bowls filled with the lamb mince, salad and garlicky yoghurt. It makes a great party, everyone stuffing their own pittas exactly the way they like them.

Makes great party food

7

Comfort eating

Food has magic powers. It can lift your spirits like nothing else – have you ever marvelled at how much better you feel after you've eaten when you hadn't even realised you were hungry? And it can grip you on many other levels too.

Proust may have famously written of the involuntary childhood memories triggered by his biting into a madeleine, but countless other writers have marvelled at how the taste and texture of certain foods can evoke memories and with them deep feelings of contentment. Our senses of taste and smell combine to help us seek out, even crave, the basic foods that we need, but it is the memories of scents and tastes that can evoke a deep sense of nostalgia. Food nourishes the spirit as much as the body.

This then is a chapter that I hope will give pure pleasure. Rich, warming lamb meatballs with evocative Middle Eastern spicing; a steak and kidney pie with a glorious crumbly crust; a Cheese, onion and bacon pie that makes my mouth water more than any other recipe; a comforting cauliflower cheese with smoky-chilli hits; a plate of slurpy noodles that will leave a chilli tingle on your lips and a warm feeling in your stomach.

These are all dishes that are most enjoyed when you are feeling low, peaky, cold or unloved. Seek solace in the act of cooking – a meditative, satisfying task – but then relish the food itself. Share it with friends, with family, even with a love, and marvel at the primal effect food can have on you. It really is magical stuff.

I first cooked this on holiday on the Isle of Mull, where the seafood is pulled fresh out of the water every day and you feel that you are on the steps of the most abundant underwater larder – it is magical. Our friends, the fabulous Avery family, wanted something different with crab, so I cooked them this: the gentle spicy flavours of the ingredients work beautifully with the delicate sweet crabmeat. I think this is one of my desert island dishes. I would happily lick the gratin dish clean.

Crab gratin

Serves 4–6

2–3 tbsp extra virgin olive oil
4 small shallots, finely chopped
2 garlic cloves, finely sliced
2 tbsp tomato purée
2 tbsp mango chutney
½ tsp mustard powder
100ml dry white wine (I like a Viognier or a dry Chardonnay) or sherry
A generous shake of Everyday hot sauce (page 176), Wahaca's chile de árbol sauce or Tabasco
A small handful of thyme sprigs, leaves picked
The brown and white meat from 3 crabs (about 800g meat)
75g stale bread, blitzed into crumbs
50g Gruyère cheese, freshly grated
50g Parmesan cheese, freshly grated

Preheat the grill to its highest setting.

Heat the olive oil in a wide-bottomed pan until gently sizzling, add the shallots and cook for 5–10 minutes until they are soft and translucent. Add the garlic and cook for another minute before stirring in the tomato purée, chutney, mustard powder, white wine, hot sauce and thyme. Simmer to reduce the wine a little and season the mixture with a healthy amount of black pepper and salt. Stir in the crab, warm through and check for seasoning, adding more hot sauce if you like.

Mix together the breadcrumbs and cheeses. Evenly cover the base of a gratin dish with the crab mix, then spread the breadcrumbs and cheese on top. Cook for a few minutes under the grill until the crumbs are crisp and the cheese has melted.

Serve with a simple watercress salad and crostini or toast.

We were staying at the Siam Hotel in Bangkok when I had my first proper pad Thai. The brilliant manager there, Jason Friedman, had invited us to a party at his house and the legendary grandmother of one of his staff came to cook her pad Thai for us. It was a lip-tingling hot, umami heaven. Although there are a lot of ingredients, once they are pulled together the cooking takes very little time. You can tone the chillies up or down very easily – a milder version is an absolute winner with the kids.

Addictive, hot, sweet and sour pad Thai

Serves 2

150g flat rice noodles
3 tbsp groundnut or vegetable oil
3 shallots, finely sliced
4 garlic cloves, finely chopped
150g raw, peeled (MSC certified) prawns
A large handful of unsalted roasted peanuts, roughly chopped
1 tsp dried chilli flakes, plus more to serve
2 eggs, lightly beaten
150g beansprouts
2 tbsp small dried shrimp (optional)
A small handful of coriander, chopped
2 spring onions, finely sliced

For the dressing
3 tbsp fish sauce
1 tbsp tamarind paste
2 tbsp lime juice (double this if you can't find tamarind paste)
2 tbsp brown sugar

To serve
1 lime, cut into wedges
 small cucumber, sliced finely

Cover the noodles with just-boiled water and soak for 10 minutes. For the dressing, mix the fish sauce with the tamarind paste, lime juice and sugar in a small bowl and set aside.

Heat a large wok until it is smoking hot. Add 2 tablespoons of oil and when hot add the shallots and garlic and stir-fry for a minute before adding the prawns and shrimps, if using, and frying for another minute. Follow with half the peanuts and the chilli and continue to stir-fry.

Drain the soaked noodles and toss well with the ingredients in the wok. Stir-fry for 1–2 minutes – the noodles will start to soften and change texture.

Now push everything over to one side of the wok. Add the remaining oil to the cleared area and crack the eggs on to it to form an omelette. When the eggs have just set break into small chunks with your wooden spoon or spatula and stir in with the noodles.

Add the pad Thai dressing and two thirds of the beansprouts, stir thoroughly and taste, adding more fish sauce, sugar or chilli, as you like. Transfer to a serving dish, scatter with the remaining chopped peanuts, beansprouts, coriander and spring onions and serve with the lime wedges, more chilli and the finely sliced cucumber.

Tip – *This recipe serves two. If you want to feed four it is better to make it in two batches or the ingredients will crowd out the wok and you won't get the same intensity of heat.*

Cauliflower cheese was one of my most dreaded foods when growing up and I seem to remember eating it a lot. Recently I was thinking back to it and wondering why I didn't enjoy it more; after all, I love both cauliflower and cheese. This is my new and improved version with the smokiness of chipotles complementing the tanginess of blue cheese. Just make sure the cauliflower is thoroughly drained after cooking; nobody likes watery cauliflower cheese!

Smoky-blue cauliflower cheese

Serves 4

1 large cauliflower
200g cherry tomatoes, halved
3 tbsp stale breadcrumbs
30g Parmesan cheese, freshly grated

for the sauce
50g butter
3 tbsp plain flour
1 tsp English mustard powder
550ml whole milk
75g extra mature Cheddar cheese, grated
50g good blue cheese like Oxford Blue
  or Stichelton
1 tbsp Chipotles en adobo (see page 169)
  or 1–2 tsp hot smoked paprika
A slight grating of nutmeg

Preheat the oven to 200°C/390°F/gas 6.

Separate the cauliflower into medium-sized florets and cut up the stalk into roughly similar sized pieces. Cook in lightly salted, boiling water for 4–5 minutes until just tender but still with some bite (you want to avoid a mush) and then transfer to a sieve so that you can drain the cauliflower thoroughly.

For the sauce, heat the butter in a non-stick pan and, when foaming, stir in the flour and mustard powder and season with salt and pepper. Stir over a medium heat for a few minutes to cook out the 'raw' flavour of the flour. Now add a good glug of milk and whisk or beat with a non-scratch whisk or wooden spoon. Gradually add the rest of the milk, whisking or beating in between additions to get a smooth, creamy sauce. Stir in the cheeses, chipotles en adobo and nutmeg and remove from heat. Check for seasoning.

Put the now thoroughly dry cauliflower in a shallow gratin dish and scatter with the tomato halves. Pour over the cheese sauce and scatter with the breadcrumbs and Parmesan cheese. Bake in the top of the oven for 20–25 minutes until golden and bubbling. Serve at once with slices of buttered brown bread.

This blissfully easy recipe is adapted from one of Madhur Jaffrey's. It takes very little time to pull together but has a wonderfully rich, exotically spiced sauce that you can mop up with simple basmati rice and naan bread. It is always a real hit when we have friends over and is yet again proof that a few spices do wonderful things to simple plates of food.

Warming cardamom fish curry

Feeds 6

7 garlic cloves, roughly chopped
5cm piece ginger, peeled and roughly chopped
2 medium–large red onions, one roughly
  chopped, the other finely sliced
1½ tsp salt
½ tsp turmeric
8 small fillets of bream or sea bass
5 tbsp olive oil
8 cardamom pods
5cm cinnamon stick
1 tsp cumin seeds
5 hot bird's eye chillies, pierced a few
  times with a knife tip
300g natural yoghurt
4 tsp tamarind paste
1 bunch coriander, roughly chopped

Put the garlic and ginger in the food processor with the roughly chopped red onion and 100ml of water and blitz to a frothy liquid. Set aside.

Rub half a teaspoon of salt and the turmeric over the fish fillets. Heat a deep, large frying pan and when hot add 2 tablespoons of olive oil. Fry half the fillets over a high heat for 3–4 minutes, skin side down, until the skin is golden and crispy. Remove to a plate and repeat with the remaining fillets with 2 tablespoons of oil. Add the sliced onion, spices and chillies to the pan with the rest of the olive oil. Fry for about 5 minutes until the onion is lightly browned, add the onion purée and a teaspoon of salt and cook for 10 minutes.

Add 250ml cold water, then stir in the yoghurt and the tamarind paste. Cook over a medium heat until warm, then slip in the fish fillets and the chopped coriander. Cook for another few minutes, then check for seasoning, adding salt and pepper if you feel it needs more. This is lovely with a bowl of rice and some stir-fried or steamed greens.

These kidneys are both savoury and sweet tasting, and because they melt and dissolve into a glorious sauce, even the most passionate offal hater will be converted. They make a wonderful wintery dinner over creamy piles of mashed potato, or an easy fast supper heaped up on toast. Despite tasting incredibly rich and extravagant you will be amazed at how little the whole recipe costs.

Balsamic lamb's kidneys

Feeds 4–6

60g butter
2 tbsp olive oil
2 medium onions, finely chopped
2 fat garlic cloves, chopped
2 chiles de árbol, finely chopped
½ tsp English mustard
A handful of thyme, leaves stripped
600g lamb's kidneys, cut into small chunks, gristle removed (ask your butcher to do this)
200ml full-bodied red wine
2 tbsp balsamic vinegar
150ml double cream
A large handful of flat leaf parsley, roughly chopped

Heat a large, heavy-bottomed frying pan over a medium heat and when hot add the butter and oil, followed by the onions. Cook gently for about 10 minutes until the onions are soft and translucent. Add the garlic, chilli, mustard and thyme and cook for another few moments before adding the kidneys. Season well with salt and pepper.

Gently cook the kidneys for about 10 minutes, breaking them up with a wooden spoon as you go, before pouring in the red wine and balsamic vinegar. Let the mixture come to a gentle simmer for 5 minutes to reduce the wine before pouring in the cream. Simmer gently for another 10 minutes until the mixture looks glossy and inviting.

Pour over creamy mashed potato or buttered toast and sprinkle over the parsley.

No one will believe how much they love kidneys!

I came up with this recipe when we were putting on our first Day of the Dead festival at Wahaca. I became obsessed with pumpkins, skeletons and all things autumnal so devised this recipe for a tea party that I was holding for my daughter. The pie looks sumptuous with its golden-orange topping and the flavours are beautifully warming when the weather gets colder.

Day of the Dead cottage pie

Serves 4–6

650g butternut or onion squash, peeled, cut into chunks
350g potatoes, peeled, cut into chunks
40g butter (at room temperature)
3 tbsp vegetable oil
65g raisins
750g minced lamb
1 large onion, finely chopped
1 large carrot, peeled and grated
2 sticks celery, finely chopped
1 tsp cumin
½ tsp cinnamon
2 tsp hot smoked paprika
2 tbsp tomato purée
A small handful of fresh coriander, roughly chopped

Preheat the oven to 190°C/375°F/gas 5.

Place the squash and potatoes in 2 saucepans of water and bring to the boil. Cook until tender then drain. Lightly mash the squash with 30g butter using a fork or potato masher. Add the boiled potatoes and continue mashing until you have a smooth purée, then season with salt and pepper and leave to cool.

Meanwhile, heat a tablespoon of oil in a large, deep casserole dish and when hot add the raisins and cook for a few minutes until just puffing up and changing colour. Remove with a slotted spoon and set aside. Add another tablespoon of oil to the pan and when hot add the meat, stirring well to break it up and brown all over, about 10 minutes. Add another splash of oil, stir in the onion, carrot, celery and spices and keep cooking for another 10 minutes to cook out the raw onion flavour. Stir in the raisins, tomato purée and 500ml water and cook for another 10 minutes.

Stir the coriander through the mashed squash. Spoon the mince into a deep oven dish and spread the mash on top. Brush the top with a little melted butter and bake for about half an hour until the top is golden and crisp. Remove from the oven, leave to sit for 5 minutes and serve.

This recipe is fool-proof and so tasty. Give it to your family as a treat one night – it makes a great change from ordinary meatballs or spag bol – or share it with friends for a cosy dinner in. They'll love the rich, warming spices and sweet-sour flavours of the tomato and tamarind sauce and you can pull it together without batting an eyelid.

Lamb meatballs with tomato and tamarind sauce

Serves 4–6

1 medium onion, quartered
1 garlic clove
1 egg
4 tbsp mild madras powder
1 bunch coriander, stalks finely chopped, leaves roughly chopped
600g minced lamb
2 tbsp olive oil

For the sauce
1 tsp cumin seeds
1 chile de árbol
2 tbsp olive oil
1 medium onion, finely chopped
3 garlic cloves, finely chopped
2cm knob of ginger, finely chopped
2 x 400g tins plum tomatoes
2 tbsp demerara sugar
2 tbsp tamarind paste

Preheat the oven to 200°C/390°F/gas 6.

To make the meatballs, place the onion quarters, whole garlic clove, egg, madras powder and coriander stalks in a food processor and season with salt and pepper. Whizz to a purée, then add the mince and pulse a few times to combine, being careful not to blend the meat too finely or into a paste. Season well with salt and pepper.

Shape the meat into 20–22 balls and place on a baking tray. Drizzle over 2 tablespoons of olive oil and bake in the oven for 15–20 minutes until golden brown.

To make the sauce, heat a deep heavy-bottomed frying pan (large enough to hold both the sauce and the meatballs) over a medium heat and when hot add the cumin and chilli. Warm them for a few minutes to release their oils before grinding to a paste in a pestle and mortar.

Pour 2 tablespoons of olive oil into the frying pan and when hot add the chopped onion and garlic, along with the ginger and crushed spices. Cook for about 10 minutes over a medium heat until the onion is soft and translucent. Now add the tomatoes, sugar and tamarind and season generously with salt and pepper.

Cook for 10 minutes, breaking the tomatoes up with a wooden spoon. Finally add the cooked meatballs and simmer for another 5 minutes so that the sauce reduces and thickens around the meatballs. Serve scattered with the coriander leaves, a bowl of hot rice and some Coriander raita (see page 172).

Get little helpers to come and
roll balls for you...

Smoky, squishy roast aubergine, fresh mint and crimson pomegranate; this is one of those recipes that not only tastes great but feels absurdly healthy. A dash of harissa brings out all those amazing flavours, but by all means add more if you like it spicier. This is fresh, satisfying comfort food, and makes a great side for a barbecue feast too.

Middle Eastern aubergine and couscous salad

Feeds 4

150g couscous
3 aubergines
5 radishes, finely sliced
2 handfuls of roughly chopped mint
4–5 spring onions, finely sliced
1 garlic clove, crushed
Seeds of ½ pomegranate
200g plum tomatoes, roughly chopped
½ cucumber, seeds removed
40g pine nuts, toasted
150g feta, crumbled

For the dressing
3 tbsp extra virgin olive oil
Juice of ½ lemon
2 tbsp pomegranate molasses
1 tbsp harissa (page 167)
1 tsp each ground coriander and cumin seeds

For the dressing, in a large mixing bowl stir the oil, lemon juice and pomegranate molasses into the harissa and ground spices and set aside.

Cover the couscous with boiling water in a bowl and then cover with clingfilm. Leave to stand for 10 minutes and then fluff up with a fork. Toss in the dressing whilst still warm.

Line your gas hob with aluminium foil and roast the aubergines over a direct flame for about 15 minutes, turning every few minutes so that they become well charred and blackened all over. They will also take on a wonderful smokiness from the flames. If you don't have a gas flame, prick the aubergines all over and grill under a high heat.

Once the aubergines are cooked lay them on a board and cut them in half lengthways, allowing you to scoop out the flesh and leave behind the blackened skin. Roughly chop the flesh and set aside in a sieve to drain off any excess juice.

Toss the couscous with the rest of the salad ingredients, finally topping with the grilled, chopped aubergine, pine nuts and feta. If you like, garnish with slivers of crispy, toasted pitta.

This is a version of a Simon Hopkinson pie, or rather a pie handed down to his mother from his grandmother. I have played with the ingredients a little but left his mouth-watering, flaky pastry as is. It is the most delicious recipe, perfect for a bleak winter's evening: the combination of fresh Lancashire cheese, salty bacon, sweet, melted onions and the bite of chilli is sensational. If you are vegetarian, by all means leave out the bacon and use shortening instead of lard, or all butter.

Cheese, onion and bacon pie

Feeds 4–5

You will need a small flan dish, about 20cm in diameter and 4cm deep (preferably with a removable bottom)

35g butter
3 large onions, halved and finely sliced
1 small bunch thyme or summer savory,
   leaves picked
1 chile de árbol, seeds removed, torn
120g rindless streaky bacon
300g Lancashire cheese (Mrs Kirkham's is a
   very good one)

For the pastry
60g cold butter
60g cold lard
a little milk, for sealing
200g self-raising flour

To make the pastry, cut the butter and lard into small cubes and rub into the flour with a good pinch of salt in a roomy bowl until the mixture resembles coarse breadcrumbs. Add 2–3 tbsp ice cold water to the mixture, just enough for the dough to come together. Knead it briefly until it is in one smooth lump and then cover with clingfilm and chill in the fridge for at least half an hour.

Meanwhile, melt 30g butter in a large, heavy-bottomed pan and add the onions, thyme leaves and torn up chile de árbol. Cook over a medium heat for about 10 minutes so that the onions are soft without allowing them to colour. Now add a teacupful of water and continue to cook for another 10 minutes. Meanwhile, add the smallest knob of butter to a hot frying pan and fry the bacon on both sides until crisp. Drain on a paper towel and then snip into small pieces onto the onion mix using a pair of scissors. When almost all the moisture in the onions has evaporated spread out the onions on a large baking sheet to cool for a few minutes.

Preheat the oven to 200°C/390°F/gas 6 and put a baking sheet on the top shelf. Butter your small flan dish and roll out two thirds of the pastry to cover the bottom and sides. Roll out the remainder of the pastry to make a lid. Spread half the onion mixture across the bottom of the flan dish, followed by half the cheese, the rest of the onions and the rest of the cheese. Brush the border of the pastry lid with a little milk and then carefully place on top of the pie, sealing the edges well with your fingers. Make a crimping pattern with a fork, create 3 slashes down the centre of the pie for air to escape and brush the lid with more milk to glaze.

Bake the pie for about 40 minutes until golden and crisp, then remove from the oven and let rest for half an hour. Serve with a crisp green salad.

Cheap cuts like chuck steak become silky and wanton after long slow cooking. Heston once told me that adding star anise to beef brings out its natural meaty flavour and, crikey, it's good! The heat from the chilli is gently warming and sparkly and the flaky, buttery pastry is a delight. As with all slow-cooks this improves hugely when prepared a day or two in advance; it also freezes well, ready to bake when you need to feed a mass of people something delicious.

A very sexy steak and kidney pie

Serves 4–6

You will need a 1.2 litre pie dish or 4 small pie dishes

3–4 tbsp plain flour
5–6 tbsp olive oil, vegetable oil or dripping, for browning
1kg stewing steak (like chuck), cut into chunks
360g kidneys, cut into chunks, gristle removed (ask your butcher to do this)
2 onions, finely chopped
3 bay leaves
1 chile de árbol (for a gentle sparkle, more if you want it spicy), crumbled
1 star anise
6 anchovies
350ml red wine
1 tbsp balsamic vinegar
2 tsp Colman's mustard
a few sprigs of thyme (optional)

For the pastry
(or buy 300g ready-made all-butter puff pastry)
160g butter
250g plain flour
A good few pinches of salt
A squeeze of lemon juice (optional)
1 egg, beaten

If making the pastry, pop half of the butter in the freezer to get it really cold. You will grate it into your pastry later to get a wonderfully flaky, buttery pastry.

Season the flour with pepper and a good few pinches of salt and place in a large bowl. Heat a large, heavy-bottomed casserole dish over a high heat and when smoking hot add a tablespoon of fat. Toss a handful of meat in the flour and brown it on all sides. Repeat with all the steak and kidneys, adding more fat to the pan for each batch. If the pan becomes too black, run a damp cloth across the bottom when you have finished browning.

Add 2 more tablespoons of fat and the onions and cook gently over a medium heat for about 10 minutes to soften. Season with salt and pepper then add the bay, crumbled chilli, star anise and anchovies and cook for a few more minutes. Break up the anchovies with a wooden spoon until they have dissolved into the onions. Add the wine, balsamic, mustard and browned meat along with just enough water to cover the meat (about 600ml). If you have any thyme, a few sprigs wouldn't go amiss. Bring to simmering point and cook over a gentle heat for about 90 minutes or until the beef is starting to fall apart. At this point you can cool and store in the fridge for a few days or in the freezer.

To make the pastry, put the flour and unfrozen butter in a food processor and blitz. Season with salt and transfer to a large mixing bowl. Coarsely grate the frozen butter into the flour and quickly and deftly stir in about 80ml of ice cold water with a fork, just enough to bring the pastry together. You want to be able to bring it together with your hands and pat it into a thickish disc. If you need a touch more water to absorb dry bits of flour add it now but remember, the less you handle the pastry, the crumblier and flakier it will be. Chill for an hour in the fridge.

On a lightly floured surface, roll the pastry to make a round or oblong 3cm wider than the pie dish you are using. Pour the meat and juices into the dish, stopping 2–3cm from the top,

then brush some beaten egg around the rim of the dish. Cut a 3cm-wide ribbon (in sections is fine) all around the pastry and lay this along the rim. Brush the ribbon with egg and fit the pastry round on top to form a lid, sealing the pastry together with your fingers and making pretty crimping shapes with a fork.

Make a slit in the middle (to allow the steam to escape), brush the top with beaten egg and chill in the fridge for half an hour to stop the pastry shrinking in the oven. Meanwhile, preheat the oven to 190°C/375°F/gas 5.

Bake the pie for 30–35 minutes until the pastry is golden and flaky and the kitchen full of enticing smells. Serve with creamy polenta or mash (pages 184,185 and 187) and a plate of greens.

8

Standby Sauces, Salsas (and Sprinkles)

This would be my choice of chapter to satisfy a committed chilli-holic. Here in a few pages is a guide to making your own sauces and salsas that can enliven and enhance food; a small collection of faithful friends that shows off the flavours of different chillies, fresh or dried, that you can keep in your fridge or larder to spice up your life.

Some of these sauces will take a bit of time. The Thai chilli jam and Chipotles en adobo weren't designed to be whisked up in an instant, but if you can be bothered to make the effort they give food rich, glorious, chilli-spiked heat and taste. Others take less time: a fiery dipping sauce here, a sticky, spicy barbecue sauce there, a hot little yoghurt number or a spicy chilli oil. Most will last for at least a week in the fridge, some for a few months.

And for an even quicker fix, why not infuse your food with a dry rub or an aromatic spice mix, or a tantalisingly more-ish mix of toasted nuts and seeds? Here are a handful of different ways to satisfy the chilli lover, whilst introducing the rich flavours that chillies bring to food.

You can buy chilli powder in supermarkets but it is hard to know when they were made and powders lose their flavour relatively quickly. There is also a rather delightful and satisfying element to homemade chilli powder, which you can use to make chilli oil (see page 163), and it makes a great present that keeps indefinitely. You can make a powder with any type of dried chilli, but some varieties are better for an all-purpose heat and taste.

Roast chilli powder

Makes a smal container

Gochugaru, Sichuan, Urfa, Aleppo or Ancho chillies
Drizzle of olive oil

Sichuan, Urfa, Ancho and Aleppo chillies all have a great flavour and won't blow your brains out. The gentle, aromatic heat of Korean chillies (gochugaru) is popular throughout many parts of Asia and these are also a great bet when it comes to making chilli powder, creating a deep lasting flavour without annihilating the tastebuds. These can be found in Asian, Mexican or Middle Eastern grocers, or online. Buy those with deep colour that also smell good.

First, snip the chillies in halves or thirds and shake them about a bit in a bowl so that you separate out as many of the seeds as possible. Omitting the seeds will make the powder more flavourful and less hot.

Open some windows and doors before starting to toast, as chilli fumes have a knack of making anyone within 100 metres cough! Heat a large frying pan or wok over a very gentle heat and toast the chillies, stirring continuously until they are crisp and aromatic. At this stage you can shake out quite a few more seeds from the bottom of the pan.

Add a drizzle of oil to the pan and continue to stir for a minute or two until the chillies slightly darken in colour.

Transfer the chillies to a pestle and mortar and grind to a coarse powder (if you use an electric spice grinder you will get a very fine powder which loses its flavour more quickly).

Tip – *Roast as few or as many chillies as you want, but bear in mind that the powder deteriorates over time, so don't go overboard.*

Having made this oil once I now find it indispensable in my store cupboard arsenal, a real heavy-hitter. It transforms even the simplest plate of food, keeps for ages and makes a great present. Toasted peanuts give the chilli oil a complexity that makes it pretty unusual. It is great drizzled over grilled prawns, chicken or lobster, or keep a bottle of it on the table for ladling over anything from tacos and tostadas to salads and stir-fries.

Hot and fiery peanut oil

Makes a large bottle

6 fat garlic cloves
25g sesame seeds
600ml sunflower oil
90g peanuts (skins on)
25g chiles de árbol (or other dried red chillies),
  stems removed
2 tsp sea salt
2 good pinches of caster sugar

Bash the garlic cloves once or twice to remove the skins easily. Heat a deep, wide-bottomed pan over a medium heat and toast the sesame seeds for 4–5 minutes until pale golden all over. Set aside.

Heat 200ml of the oil in the same pan over a medium to medium-high heat. If you heat the oil too fiercely it will burn the nuts before you manage to toast them. Add the peanuts and gently toast them until they turn a light caramel colour, turning the heat down if the oil sizzles too much.

Add the garlic to the pan and cook until it has turned soft and golden, about 5 minutes, before adding the chillies. Cook for a few more minutes until the chillies darken and smell toasted and nutty. Again, if the heat is too high, turn it down a little: if the chillies burn they will taste bitter. Add the salt, sugar and sesame seeds and pour in the remaining oil to stop the chillies cooking any further.

With a slotted spoon, transfer the chillies and half of the nuts and seeds to an upright food blender and blitz to a coarse crumb. Now add the rest of the oil and nuts and leave to cool. Store in a clean, sterilised bottle or jar (see page 179).

Make your own Chilli oil
For a simpler and more versatile Chilli oil, leave out the peanuts and finish by adding a dash of good-quality cider vinegar to the oil to bring it to life. Use this Chilli oil to add character to a plate of steamed greens or a simple fried egg, or to spice up a pizza Margherita.

A fiery little dipping sauce

The vibrant, refreshing, fiery flavours of the fresh lime and chilli in this recipe provide a terrific foil to the savoury fish sauce and the soothing, rounding effects of the sugar and garlic. It goes well with pretty much anything that has been in a deep-fat fryer and is wonderful with baked spring rolls, fried rice and noodles.

Makes a bowl

1 small clove garlic
2 fresh bird's eye chillies, roughly chopped
4 tbsp caster sugar
3 tbsp lime juice
5 tbsp fish sauce

Bash the garlic in a pestle and mortar with the chillies and sugar. Once you have a paste, work in the lime juice. Now stir in the fish sauce and check for seasoning, adding more lime juice or fish sauce to taste plus a pinch of salt if needed.

Serve at once.

Spiced seeds

These seeds make the most addictive snack you could hope to find waiting for you when you get home from work and they feel almost virtuous to eat, so packed are they with superfood staples like pumpkin and sunflower seeds. I eat them in great handfuls on their own but I also love to sprinkle them onto stir-fries and salads – they make almost anything taste better with their crunchy, salty fieriness.

Makes a small tub

50g almonds (skin on), roughly sliced
50g pumpkin seeds
100g sunflower seeds
25g sesame seeds
1 tsp olive oil
1 tsp soya sauce
1 tsp agave syrup (or maple syrup)
1 tsp miso paste (see page 21)
1½ tsp chilli flakes
¼ tsp sea salt

Preheat the oven to 160°C/320°F/gas 3.

Mix all the ingredients together in a bowl and then spread the mixture on a baking sheet lined with greaseproof paper. Cook for about 15 minutes, stirring the seeds every now and then, until the mix is dry and toasted.

Remove from the oven and allow to cool. Store in a jam jar or an airtight container where they will keep for at least 3 weeks.

Tip – *Ready-mixed packs of nuts and seeds can save you time weighing out the quantities.*

In the 1400s, spices were considered so precious that they were traded as money and sometimes worth their weight in gold. Not only did they add great depth of flavour to food, they were also valued for their healing properties before the days of modern medicine. I find they have a transformative effect on simple ingredients and, whilst there are lots of good spice mixes available to buy, their flavour can never match the taste and smell of spices that you have freshly ground yourself.

Two infallible spice mixes
– just warm and grind

Garam masala

Garam masala is a blend of spices from northern India. It normally contains black and green cardamom, black and brown cumin, cinnamon and cloves. No two spice blends are the same but their addition to dishes is supposed to intensify the flavours already present. If you wish you can buy garam masala from the shops but you will achieve a more vibrant flavour if you make your own. This makes enough for a few meals and keeps well in a small jar.

**2 tbsp cardamom pods or 1 tbsp cardamom
  seeds**
2 tbsp coriander seeds
1 tbsp ground cumin
4 chiles de árbol
5cm cinnamon stick
2 tsp black peppercorns

Warm a dry frying pan over a medium heat, add the spices and gently toast them for a few minutes, shaking or stirring the pan from time to time. Once they smell fragrant pour them into a pestle and mortar or spice grinder and grind to a uniform powder. Store in your smallest jar.

My seven-spice

I have loved Chinese five-spice powder for years; its blend of citrusy Sichuan pepper, aniseed-flavoured fennel seed, star anise and sweet cinnamon is perfectly designed for the fatty, rich taste of duck and pork. Here I have taken the original spice mix and added a touch of heat to it. It adds a delicious aromatic taste to slow meat braises or fast noodle dishes.

2 tsp Sichuan pepper
8cm cinnamon stick
2 tsp fennel seeds
2 tsp star anise
2 tsp cloves
2 tsp black peppercorns
2 chiles de árbol
3 tbsp sea salt

Warm a dry frying pan over a medium heat. When the pan is hot add the spices and gently toast them for a few minutes, shaking or stirring the pan from time to time. Once they smell fragrant pour them into a pestle and mortar or spice grinder and grind to a uniform powder, then store in your smallest jar.

Tip – *Buy spices cheaply from Asian supermarkets and make your own fresh blends – so much tastier than the bought ones!*

This harissa is a fantastically spicy paste that lasts for weeks in the fridge and peps up anything from lamb chops, sausages and grilled chicken bits to Middle Eastern salads and party food. There are many different versions but I find this has the right balance of spice and flavour.

Harissa:
a Middle Eastern salsa with heat

Makes 1 jam jar

1 red pepper, cut in half lengthways, de-stemmed and de-seeded
2 tomatoes
1 red onion
3–4 fresh red chillies
6–8 garlic cloves
150ml olive oil
3 tsp cumin seeds
3 tsp coriander seeds
1 tsp fennel seeds
A large handful each of coriander and mint
1 tbsp red wine vinegar

Preheat the oven to 200°C/390°F/gas 6.

Put the red pepper in a bowl with the tomatoes, red onion, chillies and garlic. Toss in a few good splashes of olive oil, season well with salt and black pepper and transfer to a baking tray. Roast in the oven for about 40–50 minutes until they are looking charred and softened.

Meanwhile, warm a dry frying pan over a medium heat. When the pan is hot (but not searing hot) add the spices and gently toast them for a few minutes, just long enough to unlock their fragrance. Grind to a powder with a pestle and mortar or spice grinder. When the vegetables are cooked and cool, slip the skins off the garlic cloves, leave to cool, then blitz them with the herbs and spices and stir in the rest of the oil and vinegar. Store in clean glass jars in the fridge.

Tip – *A much simpler version (albeit simpler in taste) is to whizz the chillies, garlic and spices together without roasting and store under oil in the fridge. Alternatively, there are some very good ready-made harissas in the shops, if you are short of time.*

Raisin-like pasilla chillies are not especially hot but have a dark, brooding, slightly fruity flavour that adds depth to sauces and stews. They add wonderful body to this easy chutney, which I make in the winter when I've had enough apple chutney and am looking for something a bit more complex. It goes well with a cooked ham instead of the more traditional Cumberland sauce and I also love it with cheese.

Raisin, tamarind and pasilla chutney

Makes 1–2 jam jars

30g pasilla chillies, de-seeded and torn into 3–4 pieces each
100ml boiling water
150g palm sugar or demerara sugar
50g tamarind paste (see Tip)
100ml red wine vinegar
1 star anise
4 cloves
200g raisins

Heat a frying pan over a medium heat and when hot add the chillies, stirring continuously until they smell fragrant and delicious, a few minutes. Try not to burn them or they will turn from delicious to bitter! Cover with at least 100ml of boiling water from the kettle.

Add the sugar to a small saucepan and melt with the tamarind paste. Add the vinegar, spices and raisins and let them simmer gently over a very low heat.

Meanwhile check the chilli and, when soft, blitz to a smooth paste with a stick blender. Add the chillies to the rest of the chutney and allow all the flavours to meld for 10 minutes over a low heat, seasoning well with a few generous pinches of salt. Cool, then store in a clean sterilised bottle or jar (see page 179).

This will keep for several months at room temperature but is best eaten after a few days.

Tip – *To make your own tamarind paste, take 100g of tamarind pulp and place it in a bowl with 150ml of just boiled water. Don a pair of rubber gloves and work the pulp with your hands, separating out the seeds and fibrous strings from the pulp. Push the pulp through a sieve to leave you with a syrupy, thick-ish puree which is ready to use. Store any leftover paste in the refrigerator.*

'En adobo' means in a sauce or marinade. The smoky, fiery, slightly sweet purée harnesses the intense flavours of dried chipotle chillies and is delicious in stews, pasta sauces, dressings and mayonnaises. It lasts for months and soon becomes an indispensable ingredient in the kitchen; once you start using it you may find yourself wondering how you ever did without it.

Chipotles en adobo

Makes about a litre

200g chipotle chillies (about 65)
1 whole head of garlic, cloves roughly chopped
1 large Spanish onion, roughly chopped
3 tbsp fresh oregano leaves or a few good
  pinches of dried oregano
1–2 tbsp thyme leaves
2 fresh bay leaves
1 tsp cumin seeds, crushed
4 tbsp olive oil
350ml good-quality white wine vinegar
50ml good-quality balsamic vinegar
3 tbsp tomato purée
7 tbsp demerara or palm sugar
2 tbsp sea salt

Wash the chipotles in cold water and drain. Snip off the stalk end of each chilli with scissors, which will allow the water to penetrate their tough skins. Cover with water and simmer for about 40 minutes until completely soft. When the chillies are soft, rinse off any excess seeds.

Put the garlic, onion, herbs and cumin into the blender (or use a stick blender) with 200ml water and 6 of the chillies. Purée to a smooth paste.

Heat the olive oil in a large, heavy-bottomed saucepan until it is smoking hot. Add the chilli paste and fry for about 3 minutes, stirring continuously with a spatula to prevent it catching and burning.

Add the vinegars, tomato purée, sugar, salt and another 100ml water and cook for 5 more minutes before adding the rest of the chillies. Cook for another 5 minutes, then purée the mixture before continuing to cook for 10 minutes over a low heat, stirring every so often to stop the sauce from burning. Taste to check the seasoning, adding more salt or sugar if needed.

Store in clean, sterilised jam or Kilner jars. These make great presents at Christmas.

Chipotle mayonnaise

I love mayonnaise probably more than any other sauce or dressing. I love it with chips, spread lashings on sandwiches and make tomato salads dripping in the stuff. This one harnesses the gloriously smoky flavour of dried chipotle chillies and is wonderful in the chicken club sandwich on page 130, or with deep-fried fish. It also makes a really fun and unusual pre-dinner nibble, served with little bowls of summer vegetables and some hard-boiled quail's eggs, for dipping.

Makes a small bowlful

2 egg yolks
1 tsp Dijon mustard
1 heaped tbsp chipotles en adobo (page 169)
125ml olive oil
125ml vegetable oil
3 tsp red wine vinegar
1 tsp soft brown sugar

To make the mayonnaise, put the egg yolks in a food processor with the mustard, half the chipotles and a good pinch of salt, and whizz to combine. With the motor running, slowly drip the oil through the funnel of the food processor until the mayonnaise starts to thicken and emulsify, then pour the oil in a thin stream.

Add half the vinegar and the sugar and taste (it may not need the other half). Season and add more chipotle if you like the mayonnaise spicier and smokier.

Tip – *If you are short of time, just add the chipotles en adobo to some ready-made mayonnaise and season with lime juice and a pinch of demerara sugar.*

Sticky sesame barbecue sauce

The secret ingredient in this perfect marinade is the sweet miso, which is now readily available from larger supermarkets. Its sweetness seems to accentuate the smokiness of the chillies whilst the soy adds a saltiness that renders the whole sauce irresistible. Rub lashings of this over chicken thighs or spare ribs, leave to marinate for a couple of hours (or preferably overnight) and then roast or grill. Just try it!

Makes enough for a kilo of meat

3 fat garlic cloves
2 tbsp brown sugar
3–4 tbsp chipotles en adobo (page 169)
2 tbsp miso paste
1 tbsp soy sauce
1 tbsp sesame oil

In a large pestle and mortar bash the garlic cloves together with a good pinch of salt and the brown sugar. Work in the chipotles until you have a rough paste and then add the miso, soy sauce and sesame oil.

Tip – *As you can see in the photo, this sauce is great smothered over ribs. If you fancy giving it a try, tear off the outer membrane from the ribs and lay in a baking tray with half a cup of water and bake covered for an hour at 160C, then uncover and roast at 200C for 20 minutes – yum!*

If you don't have time to make your own Chipotles en adobo you can find similar sauces in the shops. They will probably not be as good as the homemade version but they will give you the idea of smoke and heat that you are looking for.

Cucumber relish

This is a deliciously refreshing relish that you can heap onto grilled or poached fish, or barbecued chicken, or pack it into little tubs for a picnic lunch with some decent bread, cheese and ham. I love the slight kick from the chilli, but if you leave it out you will still have a wonderfully sweet-sour summer salad.

Makes a large bowl

75ml white wine vinegar
4 tbsp caster sugar
3 large round shallots
  (about 100g), finely sliced
5cm knob of ginger, finely julienned
1 bird's eye chilli, de-seeded and finely sliced
1 large cucumber, halved lengthways and
  finely sliced
A small handful of coriander, roughly chopped

Put the vinegar and sugar in a small saucepan with 75ml water and a large pinch of salt. Bring to the boil and simmer for a few minutes until the sugar has melted. Remove from the heat and leave to cool.

Meanwhile, combine the rest of the ingredients in a pretty bowl and pour the syrup over when it is cool. Leave in the fridge for 15 minutes to allow the flavours to mingle before eating.

Coriander raita

This cooling, spicy yoghurt couldn't be easier to make but it is delicious. Leave out the chillies for a more cooling effect if the food is already spicy.

Makes a bowl

A small bunch of coriander, roughly chopped
2 bird's eye chillies, roughly chopped
1 fat garlic clove, roughly chopped
250ml natural yoghurt
1 tsp sea salt

Roughly chop the coriander, chillies and garlic. Put them into a food processor with the yoghurt and salt. Blitz for a minute and then add 50ml water and blitz again. Serve with roast lamb or grilled fish dishes.

This cucumber lasts for a few days in the fridge and peps up all sorts of things

This famous Catalan sauce has travelled the globe and in every country it visits it is given a new twist. For me this makes the recipe all the more fun. What you are after is a sweet, slightly charred, roasted-tasting sauce, robust enough to transform any grilled meat but also wonderful on grilled vegetables like fennel or asparagus, dolloped over mozzarella on toast or served with anything else you fancy … I even like it on its own.

An easy romesco sauce

Makes 2 cups

2 ancho chillies, de-stemmed, de-seeded and torn into small pieces
4 large ripe tomatoes, halved
2 fresh red chillies
5 garlic cloves, skins on
130ml extra virgin olive oil
1 slice sourdough or other peasant-style bread
100g hazelnuts, toasted
1 tbsp red wine vinegar
2 tsp sweet smoked paprika
A pinch of brown sugar (optional)

Preheat the oven to 200°C/390°F/gas 6.

Heat an old frying pan over a medium heat and toast the ancho chilli pieces for a few minutes until they have puffed up a little and smell fragrant. Immediately remove from the pan so as not to burn and cover them in boiling water. Soak for 15 minutes until soft, then drain.

Meanwhile dry-roast the tomatoes, fresh chillies and garlic in the same frying pan for 15–20 minutes until the tomatoes and chillies are blackened all over and the garlic is soft to the touch. The garlic will be ready 5–10 minutes before the fruit so take them out as they soften. Set aside whilst you fry the bread.

Heat 2 tablespoons of the oil in the pan and fry the bread until it is golden. Meanwhile grind the hazelnuts and drained chillies in a pestle and mortar or food processor with the vinegar and paprika. Pummel in the tomatoes, chillies and garlic to form a rough paste and then gradually stir in the rest of the olive oil to produce a thick sauce. Season to taste with salt, pepper and perhaps a pinch of brown sugar. Don't pay any attention to the sauce separating – it will not affect the amazing taste!

Keep for up to a week in the fridge.

Tip – *In this recipe I use the sweet, deep-bodied flavour of ancho chillies but in Spain they would use the sweet-tasting ñora or guindilla peppers. If you can't get hold of any of these, use two red peppers instead – roast them in a hot oven until blackened before peeling and grinding into the sauce. If you prefer a milder sauce, leave out the fresh chillies.*

This is a chilli sauce just like Tabasco or the Wahaca chile de árbol salsa that we sell at Wahaca and elsewhere. It is relatively simple to make and thanks to the levels of heat in it (!), it lasts indefinitely in the cupboard. The oregano, cumin and vinegar add a wonderful balance of flavours to the sauce, the garlic softens the chilli kick and toasting the chillies brings out their delicious nutty notes. Leave a bottle on the table and let people help themselves – it is brilliant for perking up a plate of food.

Everyday hot sauce

Makes a large bottle

60g chiles de árbol
60ml vegetable oil
20g sesame seeds
3 garlic cloves, peeled
¼ tsp cumin seeds
1 tsp Mexican dried oregano
1–2 tsp salt, to taste
1 tsp caster sugar
½ onion
150ml good-quality white wine vinegar

Stem the chillies and shake out the seeds. Heat a frying pan over a medium heat and add the oil. When it is hot, add the chillies and toast them gently for 1–2 minutes until they darken and smell nutty. If the oil is too hot they will burn and taste bitter. Remove them with a slotted spoon and fry the sesame seeds in the same oil until they turn a light caramel colour and start to pop. Repeat with the garlic.

Transfer all 3 ingredients to an upright food blender with the cumin, oregano, salt and sugar and grind to a paste.

Finally add the rest of the ingredients to the blender and whizz for 3–4 minutes, or until you have a smooth sauce. Add 50ml water, whizz again and taste for seasoning. You may need 50ml more water to balance out the taste, and more salt or sugar. Store in clean, sterilised bottles (see page 179).

This rich tomato sauce also doubles as a simple soup. Seek out the ripest tomatoes you can find in the height of August and September, or used tinned plum tomatoes at other times of the year, and definitely don't stint on the olive oil – not only is it good for you but it makes the sauce taste silky and wonderful. As for a Spanish sofrito, you want to slow cook the vegetables for as long as possible, in order to get the most flavour from them.

A gently spiced tomato sauce

Makes lots

1.5kg very ripe tomatoes
120ml extra virgin olive oil
1 large onion, finely chopped
2 sticks celery, finely diced
1 small carrot, peeled and finely diced
4 garlic cloves, finely chopped
2 tsp chipotles en adobo (page 169) or a finely
  chopped bird's eye chilli
2 tsp ground cumin
1 tsp sea salt
2 tbsp red wine vinegar
A handful each of coriander and parsley,
  roughly chopped

Cover the tomatoes with boiling water and leave for 30–40 seconds. Drain, peel and roughly chop, making sure you catch as much of the juice as possible before puréeing in a food processor and setting aside.

Heat a large pan over a medium heat then add the olive oil. Add the vegetables and garlic, and cook over a low heat for 15–20 minutes to get the flavour from them. Now add the chipotles, cumin, a good teaspoon of sea salt and plenty of freshly ground black pepper, together with the vinegar, herbs and 500ml water. Simmer slowly for 20–25 minutes then return to the food processor to purée until completely smooth.

At this stage you have a wonderful silky tomato soup, which you can serve with croutons, chopped hard-boiled egg and diced, cured ham. To turn it into a sauce, simply return the soup to the pan and reduce by about a third.

It keeps for up to a week in the fridge, or you can bottle it by putting in clean sterilised jars.

Tip – *This sauce is delicious with pasta, mussels, chickpeas, roast lamb, gnocchi, chargrilled summer vegetables and even risotto, with plenty of freshly grated Parmesan. Change the flavour by varying the herbs. Chervil and basil are great together, as are basil and a touch of mint.*

This jam is delicious and so packed with umami flavour that it transforms anything, from fried eggs and noodles to a toasted cheese sandwich. The ingredients take a little time to prepare so I like to make this at the weekend when the weather is lousy. Rope some friends in to help (a casual invitation to lunch should do it) and you can do the job in no time. You can make them a feast afterwards, though beware of promising to give away the jam itself...

Thai chilli jam

Makes 2 jam jars

50–60g whole Kashmiri chillies (see Tip)
300ml vegetable oil
3 whole heads of garlic, cloves finely sliced
7 large banana shallots, finely sliced
5cm knob of ginger, peeled and finely sliced
1 large tbsp Thai shrimp paste
3 heaped tbsps tamarind paste
4 tbsp fish sauce
125g palm sugar (just over 10 tbsp)

Make a slit in the chillies and de-seed them. Heat a wok over a medium heat and put the extractor fan on full while you toast them – they make you cough! Add the dried whole chillies and stir continuously for 4–5 minutes until the chilli pods begin to smoke and burn in places. Remove them from the heat and allow to cool.

Add the oil to the wok and when hot deep-fry the garlic, shallots and ginger in separate batches, until golden brown. If you overcook them they will turn bitter. Fry the shrimp paste in the same oil until fragrant.

Whizz the chillies in a food processor to make a deep, burgundy-coloured chilli powder. Remove to a bowl, then whizz the garlic, ginger, shallots and shrimp paste together, using all the cooking oil to loosen the mixture.

Put the tamarind paste, fish sauce and palm sugar into the wok, add 70ml water and heat gently until the sugar has melted. Add the shallot mix along with most of the chilli powder and bring to simmering point. Taste the mixture – it should be sour, sweet, salty and spicy – then add more tamarind, chilli, sugar or salt to adjust the seasoning.

Simmer, stirring regularly, until you have a fairly thick, loose jam, about 10 minutes; it will thicken as it cools. Transfer to clean, sterilised jars (see page 179) and it will keep for months in your store cupboard.

Tip – *The authentic Thai version of this jam uses the milder, aromatic Kashmiri chilli, which you can buy at good Asian supermarkets or online. Chile de árbol is a good substitute here, but I would use half the amount so that the jam isn't too fiery.*

I like this jam with cheese, with sausages, with ham and with eggs. It is sweet, mildly fiery and full of the aromatics of ginger, star anise and the occasional explosion of coriander when you bite into the seeds. This recipe makes 2 jars but if I have time I make it in bigger batches so that I have some to give away – the jam makes great presents! Add another Scotch bonnet if you like your jam really hot.

Tomato, ginger and chilli jam

Makes 2 jam jars

1kg very ripe tomatoes, cleaned and roughly chopped
1 large onion, roughly chopped
8 garlic cloves, finely chopped
3 heaped tbsp finely chopped ginger
2 large Scotch bonnets, de-seeded and finely chopped
Juice of 4 limes
600g demerara sugar
200ml red wine vinegar
4 star anise
2 tbsp coriander seeds
1 tsp salt

Blitz the tomatoes, onion, garlic and ginger in a food processor for about 5 seconds to get a rough salsa. Add to a pan with the rest of the ingredients and bring the mixture to simmering point. Simmer, stirring regularly, for 25–30 minutes, then stir frequently for a further 15 minutes, until most of the water has evaporated leaving behind a sticky, thick jam.

You can test if the jam is ready by putting a half teaspoonful onto a saucer and placing in the freezer for a minute. If the jam wrinkles when you put your finger to it, it's ready. If not, you can continue simmering until it reaches perfection. But it doesn't really matter if the jam sets – it can be like a sticky salsa and it will taste just as good.

Spoon the jam into clean, sterilised jars, leaving a 1cm gap at the top of the jar. Leave to cool and seal tightly.

Tip – *To sterilise jam jars, put them through the dishwasher or wash in hot, soapy water, rinse well and place in a hot oven (220°C/430°F/gas 7) for 10 minutes, or fill with boiling water for 10 minutes then dry.*

9

perfect foils

A perfect foil is a complement to an already spicy dish. It is a side of vegetables or grain, of starch or greens that naturally goes well with the collection of chilli recipes that I have put together in this book. Here you will find an enticing sweet potato mash that is scented with nutty, brown butter and summery thyme; a mound of silky mash enriched with garlic and delicious olive oil; you will find polentas and quinoas designed to absorb a chilli hit whilst also giving back flavour and comfort.

In this chapter you will also find the only recipe in the book with no chilli in it – a bowl of Coconut rice that I first tried in Bangkok, which produced a powerful feeling of joie de vivre in just a few mouthfuls. You will also find a couple of lightly spiked salads: a minerally and sweet Kale and cherry tomato salad and a summery new potato salad dressed with citrus and Scotch bonnet. I hope these recipes will coax and tempt you sometimes to pay as much attention to the side dish as the main.

Travelling in Campeche, in Mexico, I discovered how incredibly well the fruity, fiery flavour of the habanero chilli goes with potatoes. This salad – a kind of English potato salad gone awry – is inspired by the potato taquito recipe we came up with at Wahaca, which is drizzled with habanero salsa. It makes a great summery side.

Warm potato salad with anchovy, habanero chilli and citrus

Feeds 4

900g waxy potatoes (such as Pink Fir or Ratte), peeled and cut into bite-sized chunks
4 anchovy fillets
1 garlic clove
1 habanero/Scotch bonnet chilli, de-seeded
Zest and juice of ½ orange
2 tbsp red wine vinegar
5 tbsp extra virgin olive oil
1 heaped tbsp mayonnaise
2 small shallots, very finely sliced
2–3 heads of chicory, leaves separated
A large handful of basil leaves, roughly shred

Simmer the potatoes in salted, boiling water for 15–20 minutes until cooked through. Meanwhile, pound the anchovies, peeled garlic clove and chilli with a good pinch of salt in a pestle and mortar until you have a smoothish paste. Add the orange zest and juice and work in; finally mix this up thoroughly with the vinegar, olive oil and mayonnaise (if it won't all fit, transfer the dressing to a small bowl).

When the potatoes are cooked, drain and, whilst still warm, toss with two-thirds of the dressing and the shallots. Check for seasoning; this type of salad needs to be well seasoned.

Toss the chicory and basil leaves in the reserved dressing and either mix through the potatoes or arrange the leaves in a pretty salad bowl topped with the new potatoes.

Go easy on the chilli – you can always add more later.

This recipe is homage to the time I spent in the Spanish Pyrenees. I remember being gobsmacked by how many ways potatoes were cooked: potato soup, patatas bravas, tortilla and this sinfully rich potato purée. Packed with healthy olive oil, it is infinitely silkier than our milky mash. I whizz it in a food processor which saves all the faff of mashing potatoes by hand – the olive oil stops the spuds going too gloopy – but mash it by hand for a lighter finish.

Spanish style mash potato

Feeds 4

6 fat garlic cloves, peeled
120ml extra virgin olive oil, plus extra for
** drizzling**
2 bay leaves, preferably fresh
900g floury potatoes, peeled and cut into
** bite-sized chunks**
5 tbsp crème fraiche
1 tbsp white wine vinegar
2 tsp sweet smoked paprika
½ tsp hot paprika

Put the garlic, olive oil and bay leaves into a small saucepan on the lowest possible heat. Warm the olive oil until a few small bubbles are breaking the surface and cook the garlic at this heat for 15–20 minutes, turning occasionally, until the cloves are soft and tender all the way through.

Meanwhile, put the potatoes into a pan of well-salted water, bring to the boil and simmer until the potatoes are cooked all the way through (test with a sharp knife – the potatoes should offer no resistance). Drain the potatoes, return to the pan and shake over the heat for a few minutes to get rid of any excess water.

Remove the bay leaves from the oil and whizz the oil and garlic in the food processor for a minute to purée the garlic. Now add the spuds and whizz for another few minutes to purée. Season well with plenty of salt and pepper, the crème fraiche and vinegar and whizz for another minute to produce a wonderfully smooth purée. The mash can keep in a warm oven for up to an hour if you cover it with another slick of olive oil and some greaseproof paper pressed against the potato.

To serve, sprinkle over the paprika followed by a good tablespoon more of olive oil.

This is a mouth-watering mash to transform a midweek supper. The caramelised flavours of the butter, maple syrup and thyme are just great with the sweet potato. I eat this with good-quality (lamb) bangers, or with the braised pork belly on page 117. For a more summery version, use olive oil instead of butter, sprinkle the mash with feta cheese, finely sliced spring onions and coriander leaf and serve as part of a mezze feast.

Sweet potato mash

Feeds 4

3 large sweet potatoes, peeled and cut into bite-sized chunks
75g butter
8–10 sprigs of thyme, leaves picked
2–3 tbsp maple syrup or soft brown sugar
1 fresh red chilli, finely chopped
1–2 tbsp soy sauce

Steam the sweet potatoes for 15–20 minutes until tender enough to mash, then drain thoroughly. Meanwhile, put a large saucepan over a high heat and melt the butter, allowing it to brown on the bottom of the pan. Once the solids have turned a deep brown, throw in the thyme leaves, maple syrup, chilli and soy sauce. Allow to bubble up for a few seconds before adding the drained, cooked sweet potato and stirring well.

Remove from the heat and mash the potato to a smooth purée. Taste and season with a little salt and pepper if you think it needs it. The mash can keep in a warm oven for up to an hour with some buttered greaseproof paper pressed against the potato.

Tip – *By toasting the butter solids you will get a lovely rich, caramelised flavour, but make sure you don't overcook it – it should be nut brown, not black.*

Coconut rice

I have never been a fan of coconut – the sight of a Bounty bar makes me shudder! – but two years ago, at a fast food joint in Bangkok, I tried a faintly sweet coconut rice, served with a particularly acidic, hot mackerel and green papaya salad, and it was so good I asked for a doggie bag to take our leftovers back to the hotel. My two-year-old tried one mouthful then polished off every last grain! Inspired by that trip, this is the only recipe in this book with no chillies, but it is included here as a wonderful foil for many of my chilli dishes. Although I am a fan of brown, red, black and brown rices, only white will do here and specifically long grain rice, which I find more delicate and delicious than short grain.

Feeds 4–6

300g long grain white rice
300ml coconut water
2–3 tbsp fish sauce
1 tsp caster sugar

Cover the rice in the coconut water and 300ml tap water, season with the fish sauce and sugar and a generous grinding of black pepper and bring to simmering point. Put a lid on the rice and cook over a very gentle heat for 10 minutes before turning off the heat. Taste the rice for seasoning, adding a little salt if you think it needs it, and cover again, leaving for another 10 minutes for the grains to absorb the rest of the liquid; they should be swollen and tender. It will not harm the rice to be left a little longer somewhere warm.

This is wonderful with almost anything, but particularly with a beef dish (see page 111) or spicy seafood. I love it so much I can eat it on its own.

Lightly spiced polenta

Grilled wedges of hard polenta don't excite me but hand me a bowlful of warm, creamy polenta, enriched with butter and Parmesan and with a little kick of chilli, and I start perking up. This is amazing with the pork on page 117 or the duck on page 114, or served in deep bowls with the delicious juices from slow-cooked meat.

Feeds 4

200g polenta
½ tsp cayenne pepper
60g Parmesan cheese
50g butter
2 tsp salt, to taste

Put approximately 1.5 litres of water in a very large pan and bring to the boil. (Different types of polenta use slightly different quantities of water so check the packet instructions for how much you need.) Add a couple of teaspoons of salt followed by the polenta and cayenne and cook over a medium heat, stirring frequently, until the polenta is starting to come away from the sides of the pan and tastes smooth and creamy.

Stir in the Parmesan and butter and serve at once.

Quinoa is an amazing grain, packed full of protein and good carbohydrates, making it a real hero of your store cupboard. Its close cousin amaranth was considered so valuable by the Aztecs that it was used as an offering to the gods; the Spanish invaders considered this heresy and every crop of amaranth in Mexico was razed to the ground. Both grains are now re-emerging in Latin America and this glorious tasting side, with its corn and chilli, is inspired by my travels there.

Buttered quinoa with sweetcorn

Feeds 4

200g quinoa
3 tbsp olive oil
1 medium onion, finely chopped
150g fresh or frozen sweetcorn
1 green jalapeño chilli, finely chopped
½ tsp ground cumin
40g butter
1 small bunch coriander, roughly chopped

Toast the quinoa in a pan over a medium heat for about a minute to bring out its nutty flavour. Pour it into a mixing bowl and set aside.

Heat the oil in a large saucepan over a medium heat and when hot add the onion, corn and chilli. Season generously with salt and pepper and sauté for about 10 minutes until the onion is soft and translucent. Stir fairly frequently so that the onion doesn't burn. Add the cumin and cook for another minute or two before adding the toasted quinoa and 500ml water.

Bring the water to the boil, season well with salt and pepper and turn the heat down so that it is simmering gently. Cook for 20 minutes until the quinoa have uncurled, releasing their tadpole-like tails, and are tender to the bite. Drain any excess water.

Stir in the butter and coriander. Check for seasoning and serve. This goes beautifully with chicken or fish, or with anything else that you might eat with rice.

Tip – *If you cannot find quinoa, a long-grain white rice will work in its place.*

I am always trying to get essential vitamins and minerals into my family's diet and spring greens are one of the cheapest and tastiest ways. Look for the tender, lighter coloured leaves; the darker, larger ones are always tougher and require more cooking. These are great with anything from sausages to grilled fish, chicken bits or steaks (see page 111). Although there seems to be a lot of chilli, when you fry the chillies whole you impart their flavour without too much of their heat.

Hot, fragrant Asian greens

Feeds 6

2 tbsp vegetable oil
5 chiles de árbol
3 garlic cloves, sliced
½ tsp whole Sichuan pepper
500g spring greens, washed, tough stalks
 removed, leaves shredded into thick ribbons
1 tsp sesame oil
A few good splashes of soy sauce

Heat the vegetable oil over a medium-low heat then add the chillies, garlic and Sichuan pepper. Cook for about a minute or until the garlic has turned a light brown colour, the chillies have lightly darkened and everything is smelling fragrant. Don't burn!

Add the greens and the sesame oil to the pan and stir-fry for 3–4 minutes until they have wilted down and are tender to the bite (the water from washing the greens will help them steam-cook).

Add a few splashes of soy sauce and season to taste with a touch of salt and pepper. Only eat the chillies if you are chilli mad!

Tip – *If you can't get hold of dried chillies use a couple of fresh red chillies, either de-seeded and finely chopped or thrown in whole. If you want a fiercer heat, break the chillies in half to release their seeds.*

When I was in LA a few years ago raw kale was all the rage. I'm not convinced by the superfood smoothie option they have over there, quite yet, but when kale leaves are young and sweet they are lovely in a salad like this, where the sweetness and softness of the cherry tomatoes contrasts so well with the fibrous, slightly minerally flavour of the greens. This is a delicious and healthy side that works with almost anything.

Kale and cherry tomato salad

Feeds 4

1 orange
130g curly kale, hard inner stems removed, leaves roughly sliced
300g cherry tomatoes, quartered
½ red onion, halved and finely sliced
1 small bunch parsley, roughly chopped
1 small fresh red chilli, de-seeded and finely chopped

For the dressing
2 tbsp red wine vinegar
1 tsp caster sugar
90ml extra virgin olive oil
1 tsp Dijon mustard

Cut the top and bottom of the orange away and, running a knife from top to bottom, cut away the skin taking the white pith with it. Now segment the orange and cut each segment into 2–3 pieces.

Combine all the dressing ingredients in a small bowl and season well with salt and pepper. Place all the salad ingredients in a large bowl, toss with the dressing and serve at once.

Tip – *Make sure you buy a lovely crisp bunch of kale – you want fresh tender sprouts not tough old leaves.*

fresh tender Sprouts not tough old leaves

10

Puddings and a few drinks

And at last to puddings! Rich, dark caramels and the sultry, fruity, notes of dark chocolate seem made for chillies, although not all of them. The concentrated flavours of dried chillies are far better matches for these sweet flavours than the high, fiery notes of some of the fiercely hot fresh chillies. I like the flavour of cayenne to add a sprinkle of heat to my puddings; or the raisin-like, tobacco tones of the pasilla to complement chocolate; even the smoky effect of the chipotle can add a subtle layer of heat to the sweetness of a pudding.

Delve into these rich and wicked desserts with gusto. Try the squidgy pasilla-spiked chocolate brownies, or the baked chocolate tart with its salty-caramelised-nutty crunch. Try the Molten chocolate, almond and espresso cake or the dark caramel of the chillied apple tart. If you want a quick sugar-chilli fix the roast pineapple with star anise is perhaps for you, or the Catalan chocolate and chilli toasts.

A few cocktails for before or after dinner may prove even more seductive. My Turkish sour, laced with the sweet-sour notes of pomegranate molasses and studded with a touch of dried chilli, is a memorable way to start any evening, but if it is a party you are after then perhaps it is the jalapeño margarita for you, a refreshing bright cocktail with a light brush of fire to wake you up – tequila is the spirit to get anyone dancing! If cocktails aren't for you, then get back to basics and curl up with a cup of my molten hot chocolate, a surefire way to cheer up a dark night.

This recipe comes from Spain and is a deeply satisfying way to start the day: a kind of super-charged pain-au-chocolat. Straddling the line between sweet and savoury, it makes a yummy breakfast with a strong flat white, or add a scoop of vanilla ice cream on top and you have a quick, easy – and totally irresistible – dessert.

Dark chocolate and olive oil toast

Feeds 4

4 slices of sourdough bread
4 tbsp extra virgin olive oil
150g dark chocolate
  (70% cocoa solids), chopped
A pinch of chilli flakes, Turkish or otherwise

Preheat the grill to its highest setting.

Briefly toast the sourdough slices so that they are a little crisp but not browned. You can do this in the toaster but it will taste even better if you pop the slices of bread on a chargrill for a minute or two a side to get that delicious charred flavour.

Drizzle the toasts with the olive oil. Arrange the chocolate on top and sprinkle with a little sea salt and the chilli flakes. Pop under the grill until the chocolate has just melted and serve as is or with scoops of vanilla ice cream or crème fraiche

Forget the instant stuff you get at children's tea parties, sophisticated homemade jellies are not only seriously good but are now all the rage. This easy, elegant and grown-up pud will have even those deeply suspicious of jellies converted in one fell swoop.

Blueberry and elderflower jelly

Feeds 4

You will need 4 small moulds, greased lightly with vegetable oil, or 4 pretty glasses

1 fresh red chilli, halved, de-seeded and diced
250g blueberries
150g caster sugar
4½ sheets leaf gelatine (enough to set 500ml liquid)
150ml elderflower cordial
3 tbsp Cointreau

Pop the diced chilli and blueberries in a pan with 300ml water. Bring to simmering point, then simmer for a few minutes to allow the chilli to infuse. Add the sugar and stir to dissolve before removing from the heat.

Meanwhile, soak the gelatine in a shallow bowl of cold water for 5–10 minutes to soften. Drain the gelatine leaves in a sieve for a minute then stir into the hot fruity liquid until they dissolve. Add the cordial and Cointreau and leave to cool.

Divide half the jelly and berries between 4 moulds or glasses and place in the fridge for 1–2 hours to begin setting. Top up with the rest of the berries and jelly and return to the fridge to set for at least another few hours but preferably overnight.

Serve with custard, cream or, to really gild the lily, the ice cream on page 205, leaving out the caramel crumbs and flavouring with Cointreau instead of rum.

easy, elegant and grown-up

This very simple fruit salad is refreshing and sweet on its own but transformed into something very special by the snowy blanket of lime and chilli ice scattered over the top. The ice is a cinch to make but it does take a little time. It is inspired by the amazing ices, called nieve in Mexico, and is a wonderful thing to whip out suddenly at the end of dinner!

Fruit salad with lime and chilli snow

Makes 500ml of nieve

2 mangoes, peeled and sliced
300g raspberries, sliced in half
150ml apple juice

For the nieve (snow)
90g caster sugar
1 fresh red chilli, halved lengthways
zest of 1 lime
100ml apple juice
150ml lime juice (about 5–6 limes)
2 tbsp 100% agave tequila (preferably an
** unaged blanco)**

To make the granita, put the sugar, chilli and 200ml water into a saucepan and place over a medium heat. Simmer, stirring, until the sugar has dissolved completely, then remove the pan from the heat. Stir in the lime zest and set aside.

Once the syrup has completely cooled down, pour in the apple juice followed by the lime juice and tequila and stir to combine. The mixture will be quite strong-tasting at this point, but once frozen it will lose much of its punch.

Pour the liquid through a sieve into a shallow dish and place in the freezer. After three hours, use a fork to break up any ice that has formed, particularly around the edges of the dish. Return the granita to the freezer, repeating the raking process every few hours or so until the whole dish consists of crunchy, flaky ice crystals. It is important to use a shallow dish, or this process will take a lot longer!

Mix the mangoes and raspberries together (you can do this a few hours before you are ready to eat, but not much longer or the raspberries will start looking soggy). When you are ready to eat, dress with the apple juice and serve in bowls with the lime and chilli snow scattered on top.

Tip – *This recipe makes enough to generously top a fruit salad or rice pudding – double up if you want more!*

These indulgent pots have an ethereal lightness and an addictiveness that I put down to the classic Mexican flavour combination of sour tamarind and hot chilli. The silky, slightly spicy tartness of the curd contrasts beautifully with the creamy underneath. What is more, you can make everything the day before.

Little lime possets with chilli-tamarind curd

Feeds 6

500ml double cream
Juice and zest of 5 large limes
150g golden caster sugar
1 tsp vanilla essence

For the curd
1 medium egg plus 3 medium yolks
finely grated zest and juice of 3 limes
4 tbsp tamarind paste (page 168)
130g caster sugar
½ tsp dried chilli flakes
150g unsalted butter, cut into small cubes

To make the posset, put the cream, lime zest, caster sugar and vanilla essence in a pan and bring to the boil, stirring occasionally to dissolve the sugar. Lower the heat and leave to bubble for a few minutes, stirring from time to time. Whisk in the lime juice then remove from the heat. Sieve the hot cream into 6–8 glasses and chill in the fridge.

To make the curd, whisk the eggs, lime, tamarind, sugar and chilli together in a saucepan over a low heat, then add the butter, one cube at a time. Let the curd cook for 10–15 minutes, stirring regularly, until it is thick and custard-like, but at the first sign of the mixture erupting with a 'plop' remove from the heat.

Strain the curd through a sieve into a clean bowl and allow to cool. Spoon a layer of the curd over each of the set possets, return to the fridge and leave to set overnight. I love to serve these with the almond biscotti on page 204 and a glass of pudding wine or aged tequila.

Tip – *This batch of curd is a little big for the recipe, so eat the leftovers on toast. Or double the recipe so that you have plenty: it's great with vanilla ice cream and will keep for a week in the fridge in a sealed container.*

Fast, easy and incredibly good, there is nothing that I wouldn't recommend about this pudding, especially when paired with a good-quality vanilla ice cream. It is marginally healthy, as far as desserts go, and is the type of thing even I can face pulling together after dinner with friends (I am the laziest person when it comes to making puddings!)

Roast pineapple with chilli syrup

Feeds 4–6

½ tsp chilli flakes, Turkish or otherwise
½ a star anise
1 clove
50g light brown muscovado sugar
1 medium pineapple, peeled, cored and sliced
   into 2–3cm wedges
80ml orange juice

Preheat the oven to 180°C/350°F/gas 4.

In a pestle and mortar or spice grinder, grind the chilli flakes and spices as finely as possible. Add the sugar and bash together to get an even powder.

Place the pineapple pieces in an ovenproof dish or baking tray lined with greaseproof paper, sprinkle with the spiced sugar and pour over the orange juice.

Roast uncovered for 30–40 minutes, basting every now and again with the syrup, until the pineapple is slightly translucent and a sticky, caramel sauce has formed. Serve straight from the oven with your favourite vanilla ice cream or crème fraiche.

Tip – *Finding a ripe pineapple makes all the difference here. To pick well, smell the bottom of the fruit – it should have a sweet, aromatic scent when ripe; if it smells of nothing, put it back and find another one if you can.*

Finding a ripe pineapple makes
all the difference here

I always feel a little virtuous when choosing biscotti instead of a pudding at the end of dinner, even though I always want to dip them into a delicious pudding wine, and there is nothing too virtuous about them in the first place. Never mind. These are wonderful, keep for ages and make the most fabulous presents, wrapped in cellophane and tied with a pretty ribbon.

Chilli and almond biscotti

Makes lots!

You will need a baking sheet (not huge!), lined with baking paper or a silicone sheet.

120g unsalted butter (at room temperature)
70g caster sugar
2 large eggs
1 tsp almond extract
220g plain flour
1½ tsp baking powder
A good pinch of salt
60g toasted almonds, roughly chopped
1 tsp dried chilli flakes
Zest of an orange
1 tsp fennel seeds, lightly bruised in a pestle and mortar

Preheat the oven to 170°C/335°F/gas 3. Cream the butter and sugar together, either in a large bowl with a wooden spoon (which requires some determined beating) or in a food mixer with a paddle. When the mixture has increased in volume and turned pale white and fluffy beat in the eggs and the almond extract.

Sieve the flour, baking powder and a good pinch of salt together and slowly incorporate into the butter mixture, finally adding the nuts, chilli, orange zest and fennel seeds.

Put the dough on a floured board and divide into 3 pieces. Roll into logs about 4cm wide and place on a lined baking tray. Bake for 30 minutes until golden then remove from the oven and allow to cool slightly.

Diagonally slice the rolls 1cm thick, lay the slices on a lined baking tray (or two) and bake until golden, about 10–15 minutes. Turn the slices over, bake on the other side for another 10–12 minutes and then transfer the biscotti to wire racks to cool completely. Hide away in a cupboard where no-one can find them.

This is my twist on the old-fashioned English pudding, brown bread ice cream, that my mother used to make when I was young. The recipe makes lots so pig out on half with the family and save the other half to give to friends for supper one night, drowned in a rich chocolate sauce. You don't need an ice cream maker and the recipe is very simple. Just remember to make the breadcrumbs in advance!

Chilli and brown bread ice cream

Feeds 8–10

You will need a baking sheet and a sugar thermometer

100g caster sugar
4 large egg yolks
1 teaspoon pure vanilla essence
750ml double cream
1–2 tbsp aged rum (depending on whether you are sharing with the kids)

For the breadcrumb praline
200g stale brown bread, crusts removed
A scant ½ tsp cayenne pepper
130g caster sugar

To make the praline, preheat the oven to 180°C/350°F/gas 4. Blitz the bread and cayenne pepper in a food processor, spread the crumbs over a large shallow baking tray and toast in the oven for 5–10 minutes, until golden brown. Leave overnight to harden.

The next day, put 100g of the sugar, and 2 tablespoons of water into a heavy saucepan and cook without stirring over a medium heat, swirling the pan to evenly distribute the melted sugar. When the caramel is a very dark reddish brown, about 5–10 minutes, remove from the heat and pour the breadcrumbs into the pan, swirling to coat. Pour onto a greased baking sheet and allow to cool before blitzing it into coarse crumbs in a food processor or pestle and mortar.

Meanwhile, put the egg yolks in a large bowl and whisk until light and fluffy. Combine the rest of the sugar with 250ml water in a small, heavy-bottomed saucepan, stir over a medium heat until the sugar is completely dissolved, then remove the spoon and boil the syrup until it reaches the 'thread' stage (around 108°C/225°F). It should look thick and syrupy and when dipped with a metal spoon the last drops of syrup will form thin threads.

Pour the hot syrup onto the yolks in a steady stream, whisking all the time, not worrying about some of the syrup flying off in all directions. Add the vanilla essence and continue to whisk until you have a thick, creamy white mousse. Whip the double cream and gently fold it into the mousse along with the rum and the caramel breadcrumbs.

Pour the ice cream into an airtight plastic container and put it into the freezer. I like to take it out half an hour before eating and serve with chocolate sauce.

Tip – *If you want to save time, cheat by buying a good-quality vanilla ice cream, stirring in the crumbs and a dash of rum whilst slightly thawed (but not melted), then re-freezing.*

This is a very naughty play on the flavours of a Snickers bar with layers of chocolate ganache, wickedly good caramel and toasted nuts. The caramel is really dark and not too sweet, flavoured with a hint of chilli and sea salt for a mysterious character.

Dark chocolate, chilli caramel and macadamia nut tart

Feeds 6

You will need a 30cm round cake tin (or two 20cm round cake tins), brushed with melted butter, and a sugar thermometer

1 quantity of pastry recipe (page 212) or 375g ready-made all-butter shortcrust pastry
1 egg white

For the chilli caramel
50g macadamia nuts
½ tsp chilli flakes
150g caster sugar
50g unsalted butter
75g soft brown sugar
3 large tablespoons golden syrup
150g crème fraiche
¼–½ tsp sea salt

For the chocolate ganache
2 eggs plus 2 egg yolks
70g caster sugar
300g dark chocolate, broken into small even-sized pieces
200g unsalted butter, diced
60g flour
A few tablespoons of cream, if needed

Roll the pastry 2–3mm thick to fill the cake tin and lift it onto the tin. Press down firmly into the sides and corners of the tin, prick all over with a fork and trim away the excess pastry, allowing for a 1cm overhang. Freeze for half an hour or chill in the fridge for up to a day.

Preheat the oven to 180°C/350°F/gas 4. Press some kitchen foil weighed down with baking beans inside the cake tin, ensuring that you fully cover the pastry. Blind bake for 25 minutes before removing the baking beans and cutting away the pastry overhang. Brush the pastry with a lightly beaten egg white and bake for another 5–10 minutes until the pastry is pale golden.

Turn the oven down to 130°C/250°F/gas ½. Heat the macadamia nuts until they are lightly toasted, then roughly chop them. Crumble the chilli into a saucepan with the caster sugar and 25ml water and place over a medium-high heat until the sugar starts to darken in patches. Swirl the sugar around to mix the dark bits into the lighter ones without stirring. Once the sugar has turned a very dark reddish brown (just before it starts smoking and turning black), add the butter and stir to mix in. Then add the rest of the caramel ingredients, except the nuts, and keep stirring to combine until the mixture has reached 110°C. Remove from the heat and stir in the nuts.

For the ganache, preheat the oven to 170°C/335°F/gas 3.

Whisk the eggs with the sugar until light and fluffy. Place the broken chocolate and the butter in a heatproof bowl over, but not touching, a pan of simmering water. When the chocolate has melted into the butter, fold in the eggs and flour. If the chocolate splits – which it will do if you have over-heated it – beat in a few tablespoons of cold cream.

Spoon enough caramel to just cover the bottom of the tin. Pour over the molten chocolate, bake in the oven for 5–10 minutes until just set, then remove from the oven and leave to cool to room temperature. Serve with lashings of crème fraiche or double cream.

Tip – *Making pastry is much, much easier than it sounds and unbelievably quick, whizzed up in moments in a food processor ready to rest in the fridge for an hour, or a few days, if needed.*

Sticky, caramelised plums with a faint bite of chilli and a light fluffy sponge cake underneath. The hint of chilli gives the plums a very light peppery taste, a little like you would season strawberries with black pepper – it's a wonderful match. Otherwise, this is the epitome of nursery food, especially when gobbled up with pools of double cream.

Plum upside-down cake

Feeds 8–10

You will need a 26cm cake tin, greased and lined with baking paper

600g plums, damsons or greengages, halved and de-stoned
250g unsalted butter
175g unrefined caster sugar
4 eggs
1 tsp vanilla extract
150g self-raising flour
100g ground almonds
2 tsp baking powder

For the syrup
100g unsalted butter
100g unrefined caster sugar
A good teaspoon dried chilli flakes

Preheat the oven to 180°C/350°F/gas 4.

To make the syrup, melt the butter and sugar in a saucepan with the chilli. Boil vigorously until they produce a thick caramel-coloured syrup and then pour into the cake tin, rotating it so that the mixture comes at least 2cm up the sides of the tin.

Cut the plums halves into four equal slices and arrange these in overlapping concentric circles over the caramel. (It's easier if you start with the outer circle first and work your way into the middle.)

Beat the butter and sugar until white and fluffy, then add the eggs, one by one, followed by the vanilla extract. Fold in the flour, almonds and baking powder and season with a good pinch of salt.

Pour this batter over the plums and bake in the oven for 45–50 minutes or until the cake is cooked and a knife or skewer comes out clean. Run a knife around the side of the tin and turn out the cake onto a warm plate, peeling the paper off the base.

This is doubly good served warm with some softly-whipped cream.

Doubly good served warm with
some softly-whipped cream

The combination of caramel and apple is a classic, but this recipe really takes it into the premier league. The apple cores and brandy provide flavouring, plus there's a brilliant little spike from the cayenne pepper to offset all that sweetness. Slice all the apples and make the caramel in advance and try it for Sunday lunch, maybe this Sunday coming up, and you'll never look back. Feel free to tone down the chilli for the nippers.

Apple tart with spiced caramel and crème fraiche

Feeds 6–8

You will need 2 large, heavy non-stick baking sheets (about 30 x 40cm)

1kg crisp apples
375g ready-made all-butter puff pastry
250g caster sugar
4 tbsp brandy
Juice of ½ lemon
100g unsalted butter
1 tsp cayenne pepper
150g dark muscovado sugar
1 egg white, beaten
200ml full fat crème fraiche

Peel, quarter and core the apples, reserving the cores, and slice into thin (3mm) half-moons. (Don't worry about the apple slices going dark; once they are cooked you won't notice this, so you can do this ahead of time.) Roll the pastry into a rectangle, the thickness of a £1 coin, and lay this on a buttered baking sheet. Prick all over with a fork then chill whilst you heat the oven to 200°C/390°F/gas 6.

Meanwhile make the sauce. Heat 125g of the caster sugar in a pan with 100ml water and the apple cores. Stir to dissolve the sugar and then simmer briskly until reduced to a thick-ish syrup, about 10 minutes. Remove from the heat, strain the syrup through a sieve into a small bowl, then add the brandy and lemon juice.

Heat the remaining 125g of caster sugar with 2 tablespoons of water and cook without stirring over a medium heat, swirling the pan to evenly distribute the melted sugar. When the caramel is a very dark reddish brown, about 5–10 minutes, but before it turns a jet black and burns (the darker you can take it without burning, the better the sauce will taste), turn the heat right down and add the apple sugar syrup, the butter, cayenne and the muscovado sugar, being careful as it will spit. Stir over a low heat until the caramel comes together, then continue simmering for 5 minutes.

Cover the pastry in baking paper and place a second flat, heavy baking tray on top. Bake for 12 minutes before removing the top tray, brushing with some beaten egg white. Bake for another few minutes, then remove from the oven.

Allow the pastry to cool a little, then lay the apple slices in 4–5 rows of overlapping moons over the top. They will shrink so overlap them well. Brush the apples with a little of the warm caramel and, when you're ready to eat, bake for 25 minutes until the pastry is golden and the apples are lightly coloured. Slice the tart into rectangles and serve with the warm caramel and crème fraiche.

If a white chocolate muffin was Dr Jekyll, this wickedly intense, smoked chilli and chocolate pudding would be Mr Hyde; in other words, it is dark, brooding and boozy and far better suited to after dinner than high tea. I like to eat it with cream or crème fraiche to temper its sultriness and a little glass of tequila on the side, as an act of sheer wantonness.

Molten chocolate, almond and espresso cake

Feeds 10–12

You will need a 23cm round cake tin and a deep roasting pan

2 dried chipotle chillies,
  de-stemmed and de-seeded
250g unsalted butter
200g light brown sugar
1 tsp vanilla extract
100ml strong espresso
350g dark chocolate, broken into small pieces
5 eggs
2 tbsp 100% agave tequila (preferably blanco)
150g ground almonds

Put the chillies in a pan of simmering water for 15 minutes to soften. Meanwhile, preheat the oven to 160°C/320°F/gas 3. Butter a 23cm cake tin and line with baking paper.

Drain the chillies then place back in the pan with the butter, 100g of the sugar, the vanilla extract, a generous pinch of salt and the espresso. Put over a medium heat to melt the butter, stirring every so often to dissolve the sugar.

Once the sugar has dissolved, remove from the heat and let the chilli infuse for 10 minutes. Then blitz the mixture with a stick blender and stir in the chocolate pieces. You may have to put the pan back over a gentle heat for a few minutes to melt the chocolate; just be careful not to heat it too much or the chocolate will burn.

Meanwhile, beat the eggs with the tequila and the remaining sugar until light and frothy. Pour the melted chocolate over in a steady stream, folding it in gently as you do so. Finally, stir in the almonds.

Pour into the lined cake tin placed inside a deep roasting pan. Fill the pan with enough boiling water to come half way up the cake tin and then bake in the oven for around 50–60 minutes until the cake is just set. It will still be very soft. Remove from the oven and leave the cake to cool in the tin and serve whilst still warm and quivering with great dollops of thick clotted cream.

*My father makes many delicious things but this treacle tart is perhaps the best.
It's one of those dishes that everyone loves, made irresistible here by the little bite of chilli
and the freshness of enough lemon to cut through all that icky-sticky sweet syrup. YUM!*

Dad's best treacle tart

Feeds 10–12

*You will need a 28cm low-sided round tart
case with a removable base*

1 chile de árbol
120g stale breadcrumbs
400g golden syrup
50g treacle
zest and juice of 1 lemon
100ml double cream

For the pastry
200g plain flour
40g icing sugar
60g unsalted butter (cold), diced
60g lard, diced
1 egg, separated

To make the pastry, place the flour, sugar, butter
and lard into a food processor and pulse a few
times until the butter vanishes into the flour.
Add the egg yolk and pulse again. In a separate
bowl, lightly beat the egg white. Save a third to
brush the pastry case and whizz the rest into
the mixture, little by little, until the pastry comes
together into a ball. You may need to add up to a
tablespoon of ice cold water to bind the pastry.
Wrap in clingfilm and chill for at least an hour.

Preheat the oven to 200°C/390°F/gas 6. Lightly
grease the tart case and coarsely grate the pastry
directly into it. Press evenly into the sides and
base, then use a smooth glass to roll the pastry

to an even thickness of about 2mm. Prick the
base with a fork and freeze for another hour.

Remove the tart case from the freezer, line with
kitchen foil, fill with baking beans and blind
bake for 15 minutes. Turn the oven down to
180°C/350°F/gas 4. Remove the beans and the
foil, paint the base with the reserved egg white
and cook for about 10 more minutes, until the
base is a pale golden colour.

Toast the chilli in a dry frying pan for a few
minutes until it has darkened in colour.
Shake out the seeds and whizz up with the
breadcrumbs in a food processor. Warm the
syrup and treacle in a saucepan and stir in the
crumbs, lemon zest and juice. Remove from the
heat, allow to cool for a few minutes, then stir in
the cream.

Spread the treacle over the tart base and
bake for 15 minutes. Turn the oven down to
160°C/320°F/gas 3 and bake another 15 minutes
or until the filling is almost set (it will harden
as it cools). Serve the warm tart with vanilla
ice cream or double cream or – if you are my
father – both!

Tip – *The tart is lovely eaten warm but it is also
delicious the next day with some cold cream
poured on top.*

The deep fruity flavours of the pasilla chilli match, and even enhance, those same flavours in the chocolate, meaning that these gloriously squidgy, rich squares of fudge brownie will make you the most popular person at whatever party, picnic or festival you go to. If you don't have any pasilla you can always fudge it (tee hee) with a few pinches of cayenne, but you will be seriously missing out, and they are easy to find online (see page 220).

Chocolate and pasilla chilli fudge brownies

Feeds 10–12

You will need a 23cm cake tin, lined with baking paper

250g golden caster sugar
250g butter
15g pasilla chilli flakes (see Tip)
250g chocolate (70 per cent cocoa solids)
3 large eggs plus 1 egg yolk
65g flour
60g finest quality cocoa powder
½ tsp baking powder

Preheat the oven to 180°C/350°F/gas 4.
Beat the sugar and butter for 5 minutes until pale and fluffy. Toast the chilli flakes briefly in a dry, medium-hot frying pan, before grinding them to a powder in a pestle and mortar or spice grinder. Meanwhile, break the chocolate into pieces. Chop 50g into very small chunks and set aside. Melt the rest in a heatproof bowl over, but not touching, a pan of simmering water. Remove from the heat.

Break the eggs into a small bowl and beat them lightly with a fork. Sift together the flour, cocoa, chilli and baking powder. Beat the eggs into the sugar mixture bit by bit until fully incorporated, then stir in the melted chocolate with a large metal spoon. Season with a good pinch of salt, then fold in the chocolate chunks and the flour until fully combined.

Use a spatula to scoop the mixture into the baking tin, smooth the top over and bake in the oven for 25 minutes. Test with a thin skewer. If there is a lot of wet cake mixture clinging to it, bake the cake for another 3 minutes and try again. If a tiny amount is visible on the skewer the brownies are ready (they carry on cooking once out of the oven). Keep checking every 3 minutes until you have them right. The brownies should be soft and gooey (but not runny) in the middle and feel a little spongey on the surface.

Tip – *You can buy pasilla chillies already de-seeded and in flakes but if you buy them whole, simply de-stem, de-seed and then weigh the amount stated before tearing into pieces.*

The Aztecs and Miztecs drank a savoury, spiced hot chocolate before going into battle.
Such was the powerful charge it gave the drinker that only noblemen and kings were allowed it.
This recipe is a richly potent, silky smooth chocolate hit, with the raisin-like flavour of the pasilla
chillies bringing out all the naturally fruity flavours of the chocolate. So good is the combined effect
of the cacao and the sugar that it has ruined me for life.

My molten hot chocolate

Makes 2 small cups

2 tsp best-quality cocoa powder
300ml whole milk
1 tsp pasilla chilli flakes or a tiny sprinkle
  of cayenne pepper
1 tsp brown sugar
40g dark chocolate (70% cocoa solids),
  roughly chopped
A pinch of cinnamon

Mix the cocoa powder into a smooth paste with a tablespoon of milk, then add another tablespoon to thin it down a little more. Put the rest of the milk and the chilli flakes in a small saucepan over a low heat and bring to simmering point.

Let the chillies steep in the milk for 5 minutes. At this point you can strain the milk but I prefer to keep all the flavour of the chilli in the drink so I combine the cocoa paste with the hot milk and whizz with a stick blender. Pour this back into the pan along with the sugar, chocolate and cinnamon and heat gently, stirring continuously, to melt the chocolate, being careful not to let it burn.

Retreat to a quiet corner and let the chilli chocolate work its magic.

Tip – *Try to buy the best quality cocoa powder you can find (it does make a difference) and of course a dark chocolate that you love.*

Lemongrass has a fresh, citrusy flavour that brings Thai curries alive but also makes wonderful puddings and syrups. Here I take a basic sugar syrup and breathe a South East Asian character through it with hints of chilli, ginger and lemongrass. This is a long and cool drink that should quench your thirst on hot, balmy days. A funky Antiguan granny was the inspiration behind it.

Tiggy G's gin fizz

Makes 2

80ml good-quality gin
60ml freshly squeezed lemon juice
sparkling water

For the lemongrass syrup
3 sticks lemongrass, bashed
10 thin slices of ginger
1 chile de árbol, broken up
200g demerara sugar

To make the syrup, put the lemongrass, ginger and chile de árbol in a small saucepan with the sugar and 250ml water. Bring to the boil and simmer very gently for 10 minutes by which time the sugar will have melted and the syrup will be infused with the other ingredients.

Shake the gin, lemon juice and 60ml of the lemon grass syrup over ice in a cocktail shaker. Pour into tall highballs filled with ice and top with sparkling water. Serve at once.

Tip – *Sugar syrup is used to sweeten cocktails. To make it, dissolve equal quantities of caster sugar and water, then cool before adding a teaspoon to your cocktail. Keep the syrup in a clean, sterilised jar in the fridge or drinks cupboard – it always comes in handy.*

Being a massive fan of 100% agave tequila, it goes without saying that I am also a huge fan of a margarita, probably one of the best cocktails ever invented. This elegant adaptation has the light summery feel of cucumber and mint to bring the margarita firmly into an English setting, with the wonderfully tingly spiciness of the jalapeño to keep that Mexican edge. The result is a harmonious and addictive cocktail that manages to be subtle, spicy and fresh all in one sip.

Cucumber and jalapeño margarita

Makes 2

175g cucumber, a couple of slices reserved, the rest roughly chopped
20g jalapeño chilli, de-stemmed, de-seeded and roughly chopped
50ml lime juice, freshly squeezed
25ml sugar syrup (page 216)
70ml apple juice
10 mint leaves
60ml tequila blanco 100% agave

Blitz the cucumber, chilli, lime juice and sugar syrup together in an upright blender. Slowly pour in the apple juice to purée the cucumber and chilli as finely as possible.

With a rolling pin or professional drinks muddler, muddle the mint in the bottom of a cocktail shaker to bring out its oils. Pour in the puréed liquid and tequila and shake over ice.

Pour through a fine sieve (or a professional Hawthorn strainer) into glasses that you have chilled in the freezer. Garnish with a slice of cucumber.

Nearly Virgin Mary

A Bloody Mary is probably one of the best drinks in the world. I am also partial to a Virgin Mary, which I drink all the time – it takes the edge off being hungry when I am close to lunch, feels fairly healthy and has a decent smattering of chilli to keep me on my toes. At home, we add sherry and red wine to our Virgin Mary, which renders it totally delicious, if not completely innocent. But if my daughter Tati is around we skip the alcohol because it seems to be her favourite drink too. She has immaculate taste.

Makes a large jug

1.5 litres tomato juice, chilled
juice of 1 lemon
1 tbsp Worcestershire sauce
1 tsp Everyday hot sauce (page 176),
  Tabasco or Wahaca's chile de árbol sauce
Several good grindings of pepper
½ tsp celery salt
1 tsp flaky sea salt
100ml beef consommé
50ml sherry
100ml red wine
Celery sticks, to garnish

Combine all of the ingredients in a jug and stir well. Taste and adjust the balance of spicy, savoury and sour with Tabasco, salt and lemon, as you like. Serve the Virgin Mary in highballs filled to the brim with ice, and add a celery stick and a good grinding of black pepper to garnish.

Tip – *If you want to make Bloody Marys, pour 40ml vodka into a highball, fill to the brim with ice and fill with the Virgin Mary mix. Adapt to your taste.*

Turkish sour

Whisky sour was one of the first cocktails I discovered, thanks to my grandmother from Tennessee and her infinite appetite for cocktails and fun. Whilst living in Chile I discovered the Pisco sour, which is almost as delicious, with the same vibrancy of flavour from the pisco brandy, fresh lemon juice and sugar. Bourbon sour came next, a slightly sweeter version than whisky. And Turkish sour was the obvious next step, after falling for the slightly sweet, smoky flavour of Turkish chilli flakes on a recent trip to Istanbul. The pomegranate molasses intensify the balance between sweet and sour that I find so more-ish in a cocktail.

Makes 2

1 egg white (optional)
75ml bourbon
60ml freshly squeezed lemon juice
2 tbsp pomegranate molasses
25ml sugar syrup (page 216)
Turkish chilli flakes

Beat the egg white, if using, and add it to a cocktail shaker with the vodka, lemon juice, molasses and sugar syrup. Shake hard over lots of ice and serve straight up in chilled cocktail glasses, dusted with a hint of Turkish chilli.

Tip –*With all sours I add an egg white, which makes for a smooth, savoury finish, but if you worry about raw egg you can leave it out. A non-traditional garnish is a maraschino cherry, which I love, philistine that I am. If you can't get hold of Turkish chilli flakes add a dusting of hot (or sweet if you prefer) smoked paprika instead.*

Stockists

I think the UK is one of the easiest places to buy exotic ingredients thanks to our hugely diverse ethnic makeup. Particular towns and cities will have greater numbers of specialist Middle Eastern, Chinese or Asian grocers depending on their ethnicities but what you can't find locally you should be able to find on the internet. For fresh ingredients like lemongrass, galangal, kaffir lime leaves, curry leaves, Sichuan pepper and chillies buy more than you need and freeze the surplus in well-sealed plastic tubs. Well-stocked Asian grocers sell increasingly good-quality chilli powders and flakes, if you can't find the time to make your own. If you want to explore chillies further have a look at some of the specialist online suppliers listed below, and order chilli varieties that you have not come across before. Mexican chillies are easy to buy online and are increasingly available from better-stocked supermarkets too. Unlike chilli powder, whole dried chillies keep well for a year to 18 months. You can tell when they are starting to deteriorate as their skin loses its suppleness and they turn brittle and dry and crumble easily. Avoid the menacingly small Indian and Thai chillies, as these are pretty damn hot. Here are some stockists to get you started.

The Asian Cookshop is a great supplier of Thai, Indian and Chinese ingredients and harder to find sauces like kecap manis and sambal oelek.
www.theasiancookshop.co.uk

Brindisa for a range of Spanish food, including beautiful, fresh chorizo as well as guindillas and choricero peppers and sweet and spicy smoked paprika.
www.brindisa.co.uk

Casa Mexico, 'purveyors of the finest products from Mexico,' offer a rich variety of dried chillies (árbol, chipotle, pasilla etc.), plus tortillas, beans, totopos, salsas and more.
www.casamexico.co.uk

Chilli Pepper Pete opened one of the UK's first chilli shops, in Brighton, and started the National Chilli Awards. They stock a range of award winning sauces, dried chillies, pastes, blends and seeds.
www.chillipepperpete.com

Edible Ornamentals were the first British farm to do pick-your-own chillies and sell all kinds of chilli-related goodies, including their own range of hot sauces. Check out their award-winning produce online.
www.edibleornamentals.co.uk

El Azteca was created by Mexicans for Mexicans, so the website is in Spanish, but if you are interested in any of the products, you can get the Google translation.
www.elaztecafood.co.uk

Fire Foods, a family business from Grantham Lincolnshire, broke the Guinness World Record in 2011 by growing the world's hottest ever chilli, the Infinity chilli. Order the seeds to grow your own or choose from a range of wickedly hot sauces.
www.firefoods.co.uk

Lupe Pinto's Deli has outlets in both Edinburgh and Glasgow, as well as an online shop featuring a range of imported Mexican sauces and groceries, herbs and spices.
www.lupepintos.com

Mmm… stocks some lovely food produce, including a wide range of chillies, chilli chutneys and harder to find spices. Shop online or find mmm… at the Grainger Market Arcade in Newcastle. They are alive on twitter, where I first found them.
www.mmm-food.co.uk

Peppers by Post chillies are grown by Michael and Joy Michaud at Sea Spring Farm in rural Dorset and are sold during the harvest season, from late July to early December. Order a mixed bag and you could become an aficionado!
www.peppersbypost.biz

Seasoned Pioneers have been around since I first started working in food and not only stock a huge range of spices but also a wonderfully diverse range of spice pastes and blends. The packets are small but beautiful.
www.seasonedpioneers.co.uk

The Spicery is an excellent resource for chillies and spices with detailed descriptions of all the different ones you are buying.
www.thespicery.com

Sous Chef is a new and brilliant stockist of every ingredient you'll ever need in the kitchen. A game changer.
www.souschef.co.uk

South Devon Chilli Farm is an amazing resource of fresh chillies, dried chillies, chilli sauces, chilli chocolates and chilli jellies. Over 10,000 chilli plants grow here each year, so you shouldn't be stumped for inspiration!
www.southdevonchillifarm.co.uk

The Spice Shop in London is worth a visit for its wide selection of chillies, both fresh and dried but beware, its prices are out of this world!
www.thespiceshop.co.uk

Thai Food Online for all things Thai.
www.thai-food-online.co.uk

Wally's Delicatessen in Wales stock a selection of chillies, pickled jalapeños, cooking chorizo and cider vinegar.
www.wallysdeli.co.uk

Wing Yip is the place for exotic Chinese and Southeast Asian ingredients like Shaoxing rice wine and chilli bean paste.
www.wingyipstore.com

World of Chillies offers you the chance to grow your own chillies from seed, as well as selling a variety of fresh and dried chillies to capture the imagination.
www.worldofchillies.com

Index

Almonds
Almond, apricot and carrot pilau 90
Chilli and almond biscotti 204
molten chocolate, almond and espresso cake 211
Warm Indian quinoa salad with whiting, grapes and almonds 108
American chilli beef 99
Anchovies
Spaghetti with lemon, anchovy, spinach and capers 54
Warm potato salad with anchovy, habanero chilli and citrus 182
Apple tart with spiced caramel 210
Apricots
Almond, apricot and carrot pilau 90
Asian slow-cooked pork belly 117
Asparagus
Broad bean, asparagus, fennel and green bean summer stew 102
Chargrilled asparagus with salsa verde 28
Aubergines
Middle eastern aubergine and couscous salad 156
Sichuan aubergines with ginger, garlic and chilli 88
Avocados
Avocado salsa 64
Caramelised scallop, avocado and orange salad 32
Corn, fennel, rocket and avocado salad 31
Creamy green gazpacho with spinach and avocado 62
Prawn tostadas with avocado 34

Bacon
Cheese, onion and bacon pie 157
Orange-spiced french toast with bacon and maple syrup 124
Beans
Homemade baked 86
See also individual types of bean
Beef
American chilli beef 99
Shin of beef with pasilla chilli, rosemary and prunes 140
Stir-fried minced beef with Thai basil 59
Thai style grilled beef with a quinoa and cherry tomato salad 111
A very sexy steak and kidney pie 158–9
Beetroot
My mother's amazing beetroot, parsnip and horseradish soup 68
Biscotti, chilli and almond 204
Black pudding and chicory salad with roast pear and paprika 40
Blueberry and elderflower jelly 196
Borlotti beans with spinach, sage, burnt butter and cayenne 87
Bread
Braised fennel and mascarpone bruschetta 26
Chilli and brown bread ice cream 205

Dark chocolate and olive oil toast 194
Gently spiced mushrooms on toast 44
Orange-spiced french toast with bacon and maple syrup 124
Peach, cured ham and mozzarella bruschetta 24
The ultimate chicken club sandwich 130
Welsh rarebit and leek sandwiches 80
Brill with potatoes, black olives, orange and fennel 105
Broad bean, asparagus, fennel and green bean summer stew 102
Broccoli, spicy Sichuan noodles with tofu and 51
Brownies, chocolate and pasilla chilli fudge 214
Bruschetta
Braised fennel and mascarpone 26
Peach, cured ham and mozzarella 24

Cakes
Chocolate and pasilla chilli fudge brownies 214
Molten chocolate, almond and espresso cake 211
Plum upside-down cake 208
Caramel
Apple tart with spiced caramel 210
Dark chocolate, chilli caramel and macadamia nut tart 206–7
Duck breast with caramel seven-spice sauce 114
Carrots
Almond, apricot and carrot pilau 90
Cauliflower
Penne with fried cauliflower, raisins and pine nuts 48
Smoky-blue cauliflower cheese 148
Spiced cauliflower soup with avocado salsa 64
Cheese
Cheese, onion and bacon pie 157
Feta, watermelon and pitta crisp salad 136
Peach, cured ham and mozzarella bruschetta 24
Roasted red pepper and goat's cheese tart 94
Smoky-blue cauliflower cheese 148
Spinach pastilla pie 126
Twice-baked goat's cheese and fennel souffle with hazelnut crust 30
Welsh rarebit and leek sandwiches 80
See also mascarpone
Chicken
Chicken, coconut and lemongrass soup 71
Chicken piri piri with new potatoes, red peppers, oregano and lemon 75
Chicken schnitzel with fresh tomato and chilli salad 106
Grilled Malaysian-style chicken 132
Spicy, fragrant chicken with chilli, ginger and peanuts 96
Super-fast chicken-fried rice 58
The ultimate chicken club sandwich 130

Chicken livers
Warm spiced lentils and rice with chicken livers, lemon and pomegranate 92
Chickpeas
Chickpea and mango salad with Indian spices 27
Tuscan chickpea and vegetable soup 67
Chicory
Black pudding and chicory salad with roast pear and paprika 40
Chilli and almond biscotti 204
Chilli and brown bread ice cream 205
Chillies
Dicing and slicing 19
Dried 15, 19
Fresh 16
Hand washing 19
Health benefits 7–8
Origin 8, 11
Testing for heat 11, 18
Types of 12–17
Chipotle mayonnaise 170
Chipotles en adobo 169
Chocolate
Chocolate and pasilla chilli fudge brownies 214
Dark chocolate and olive oil toast 194
Dark chocolate, chilli caramel and macadamia nut tart 206–7
Molten chocolate, almond and espresso cake 211
My molten hot chocolate 215
Chorizo
chorizo, new potato and chile de árbol pizza 134
Sweetcorn and chorizo fritters 128
Chutney, raisin, tamarind and pasilla 168
Coconut
Chicken, coconut and lemongrass soup 71
Coconut milk
Thai red curry coconut prawns 110
Coconut rice 187
Coffee
molten chocolate, almond and espresso cake 211
Coriander raita 172
Couscous
Middle eastern aubergine and couscous salad 156
Crab
Crab gratin 144
Thai crab salad with Nam Jim dressing 39
Cress, tonnata with egg and 129
Cucumber
Cucumber and jalapeño margarita 217
Cucumber relish 172
Curries
Potato, pea and ginger 82
Thai red curry coconut prawns 110
Warming cardamom fish curry 150

Dad's best treacle tart 212
Day of the dead cottage pie 152

Duck
Duck breast with caramel
    seven-spice sauce 114

Eggs
Tonnata with egg and cress 129
Turkish eggs 84
Elderflowers
Blueberry and elderflower jelly 196

Fennel
Braised fennel and mascarpone
    bruschetta 26
Brill with potatoes, black olives, orange
    and fennel 105
Broad bean, asparagus, fennel and
    green bean summer stew 102
Corn, fennel, rocket and avocado
    salad 31
Falling apart lentils with sweet fennel 91
Twice-baked goat's cheese and fennel
    soufflé 30
Fish
a simple Spanish fish stew 72
Warming cardamom fish curry 150
See also anchovies, mackerel, etc
French toast, orange-spiced 124
Fritters, sweetcorn and chorizo 128
Fruit salad with lime and
    chilli snow 198

Garam masala 166
Gazpacho with spinach and avocado 62
Gin
Tiggy G's gin fizz 216
Ginger
Potato, pea and ginger curry 82
Sichuan aubergines with ginger,
    garlic and chilli 88
Spicy, fragrant chicken with chilli,
    ginger and peanuts 96
Tomato, ginger and chilli jam 179
Goan-spiced mackerel 54
Grapes
Warm Indian quinoa salad with whiting,
    grapes and almonds 108
Green beans
Broad bean, asparagus, fennel and
    green bean summer stew 102
Gremolata, black risotto with
    squid ink and 104

Ham
Peach, cured ham and mozzarella
    bruschetta 24
Harissa 167
Horseradish
My mother's amazing beetroot, parsnip
    and horseradish soup 68

Ice cream, chilli and brown bread 205
Indian quinoa salad 108

Jam
Thai chilli 178
Tomato, ginger and chilli 179
Jelly, blueberry and elderflower 196

Kale and cherry tomato salad 190
Kidneys
A very sexy steak and kidney pie 158–9

Lamb
Day of the dead cottage pie 152
Lamb meatballs with tomato and
    tamarind sauce 154
Lebanese lamb wraps 137
Middle eastern rose-scented,
    falling apart lamb 120
Lamb's kidneys, balsamic 151
Lebanese lamb wraps 137
Leeks welsh rarebit and
    leek sandwiches 80
Lentils
Falling apart lentils with sweet fennel 91
Warm spiced lentils and rice
    with chicken livers, lemon and
    pomegranate 92
Limes
Lime and chilli snow 198
Little lime possets with
    chilli-tamarind curd 200

Macadamia nuts
Dark chocolate, chilli caramel and
    macadamia nut tart 206–7
Mackerel, goan-spiced 54
Malaysian-style chicken, grilled 132
Mangoes
Chickpea and mango salad 27
Margarita, cucumber and jalapeño 217
Mascarpone
Braised fennel and mascarpone
    bruschetta 26
Mayonnaise, chipotle 170
Middle eastern aubergine and
    couscous salad 156
Middle eastern rose-scented, falling
    apart lamb 120
Mushrooms
Gently spiced mushrooms on toast 44
Mussels, Southern Indian rasam
    soup with 70

Nearly virgin Mary 218
Noodles
Addictive, hot, sweet and sour
    pad Thai 146
Spicy Sichuan noodles with tofu
    and broccoli 51

Olives
Brill with potatoes, black olives,
    orange and fennel 105
Orecchiette with cherry tomatoes
    and black olives 50
Oranges
Brill with potatoes, black olives,
    orange and fennel 105
Caramelised scallop, avocado
    and orange salad 32
Orange-spiced french toast with
    bacon and maple syrup 124

Pad Thai addictive, hot, sweet
    and sour 146
Parsnips
My mother's amazing beetroot, parsnip
    and horseradish soup 68
Pasta
Cheat's pumpkin ravioli 52
Linguine with a deliciously spicy
    pumpkin seed pesto 46
Orecchiette with cherry tomatoes
    and black olives 50
Penne with fried cauliflower, raisins
    and pine nuts 48
Spaghetti with lemon, anchovy,
    spinach and capers 54
Peach, cured ham and mozzarella
    bruschetta 24
Peanuts
Addictive, hot, sweet and sour
    pad Thai 146
Hot and fiery peanut oil 163
Spicy, fragrant chicken with chilli, ginger
    and peanuts 96
Pears
Black pudding and chicory salad
    with roast 40
Peas
Potato, pea and ginger curry 82
Peppers
Chicken piri piri with new potatoes,
    red peppers, oregano and lemon 75
Roasted red pepper and goat's
    cheese tart 94
Stuffed peppers with pork, smoked
    paprika and thyme 125
Pesto, pumpkin seed 46
Pies
Cheese, onion and bacon 157
Spinach pastilla 126
A very sexy steak and kidney 158–9
Pineapple
Roast pineapple with chilli syrup 202
Pitta bread
Feta, watermelon and pitta crisp
    salad 136
Pittas stuffed with potato, pea and
    ginger curry 82
Pizza, chorizo, new potato and
    chile de árbol 134
Plum upside-down cake 208
Polenta, lightly spiced 187
Pomegranates, warm spiced lentils and
    rice with chicken livers, lemon and 92
Pork
Addictive pork laab salad 118
Asian slow-cooked pork belly 117
Stuffed peppers with pork, smoked
    paprika and thyme 125
Possets
Little lime possets with chilli-tamarind
    curd 200
Potatoes
Baked potatoes with American
    chilli beef 99
Brill with potatoes, black olives,
    orange and fennel 105
Chicken piri piri with new potatoes, red
    peppers, oregano and lemon 75

Chorizo, new potato and chile
  de árbol pizza 134
Day of the dead cottage pie 152
Potato, pea and ginger curry 82
Spanish style mash potato 184
Warm potato salad with anchovy,
  habanero chilli and citrus 182
Prawns
Prawn tostadas with avocado and
  spicy peanut oil 34
Thai red curry coconut prawns 110
**Prunes, shin of beef with pasilla
  chilli, rosemary and 140**
Pumpkin
Thai style spicy pumpkin soup 66
Pumpkin seed pesto 46

Quinoa
Buttered quinoa with sweetcorn 188
Quinoa and cherry tomato salad 111
Warm Indian quinoa salad with whiting,
  grapes and almonds 108

Rabbit
Pot roast rabbit with oregano
  and mustard 116
Radicchio
Risotto with chilli, radicchio and
  sausage 76
**Raisin, tamarind and pasilla
  chutney 168**
Raita, coriander 172
Relish, cucumber 172
Rice
Almond, apricot and carrot pilau 90
Black risotto with squid ink
  and gremolata 104
Coconut rice 187
Risotto with chilli, radicchio and
  sausage 76
Super-fast chicken-fried rice 58
Warm spiced lentils and rice
  with chicken livers, lemon and
  pomegranate 92

Salads
Addictive pork laab 118
Black pudding and chicory salad
  with roast pear and paprika 40
Caramelised scallop, avocado
  and orange 32
Chickpea and mango salad 27
Corn, fennel, rocket and avocado 31
Feta, watermelon and pitta crisp 136
Fruit salad with lime and chilli snow 198
Kale and cherry tomato 190
Middle eastern aubergine and
  couscous 156
Quinoa and cherry tomato 111
Thai crab salad 39
Tomato and chilli 106
Warm Indian quinoa salad 108
Warm potato salad 182
Salmon and spring green stir-fry 56
Salsa, avocado 64
**Salsa verde, chargrilled asparagus
  with 28**

Sandwiches
The ultimate chicken club 130
Welsh rarebit and leek 80
Sauces
Caramel seven-spice 114
An easy romesco 174
Everyday hot 176
A fiery little dipping 164
A gently spiced tomato 177
Sticky sesame barbecue 170
Tomato and tamarind 154
**Sausages, risotto with chilli,
  radicchio and 76**
Scallops
Caramelised scallop, avocado and
  orange salad 32
Schnitzels, chicken 106
Seeds, spiced 164
**Sichuan aubergines with ginger,
  garlic and chilli 88**
Sichuan chilli bean paste 21
**Sichuan noodles with tofu and
  broccoli 51**
**Soufflé, twice-baked goat's cheese
  and fennel 30**
Soups
Chicken, coconut and lemongrass 71
Creamy green gazpacho 62
My mother's amazing beetroot, parsnip
  and horseradish 68
Southern Indian rasam soup with
  mussels 70
Spiced cauliflower soup 64
Thai style spicy pumpkin 66
Tuscan chickpea and vegetable 67
**Southern Indian rasam soup
  with mussels 70**
Spanish fish stew 72
Spanish smoked paprika 17
Spanish style mash potato 184
Spices
Spiced seeds 164
Two infallible spice mixes 166
Spinach
Borlotti beans with spinach, sage, burnt
  butter and cayenne 87
Creamy green gazpacho with spinach
  and avocado 62
Spaghetti with lemon, anchovy,
  spinach and capers 54
Spinach pastilla pie 126
Spring greens
Easy-peasy salmon and spring
  green stir-fry 56
Hot, fragrant Asian greens 189
Squash
Cheat's pumpkin ravioli 52
Squid, salt and pepper 36
Squid ink
Black risotto with squid ink
  and gremolata 104
Steak and kidney pie 158–9
Stews
Broad bean, asparagus, fennel and
  green bean summer 102
A simple Spanish fish stew 72
Stir-fries
Easy-peasy salmon and spring green 56

Stir-fried minced beef with Thai basil 59
Super-fast chicken-fried rice 58
Store cupboard 20–1
Sweet potato mash 185
Sweetcorn
Buttered quinoa with 188
Corn, fennel, rocket and avocado
  salad 31
Sweetcorn and chorizo fritters 128
Syrup, chilli 202

Tamarind
Chilli-tamarind curd 200
Raisin, tamarind and pasilla chutney 168
Tomato and tamarind sauce 154
Tarts
Apple tart with spiced caramel 210
Dad's best treacle 212
Dark chocolate, chilli caramel and
  macadamia nut 206–7
Roasted red pepper and goat's cheese 94
Thai chilli jam 178
Thai crab salad 39
Thai red curry coconut prawns 110
Thai style grilled beef 111
Thai style spicy pumpkin soup 66
Tiggy g's gin fizz 216
Tofu
Spicy Sichuan noodles with tofu
  and broccoli 51
Tomatoes
Creamy green gazpacho with
  spinach and avocado 62
A gently spiced tomato sauce 177
Homemade baked beans 86
Kale and cherry tomato salad 190
Nearly virgin Mary 218
Orecchiette with cherry tomatoes
  and black olives 50
Quinoa and cherry tomato salad 111
Tomato and chilli salad 106
Tomato and tamarind sauce 154
Tomato, ginger and chilli jam 179
Turkish eggs 84
Tonnata with egg and cress 129
Tostadas
Prawn tostadas with avocado and
  spicy peanut oil 34
Treacle
Dad's best treacle tart 212
Tuna
tonnata with egg and cress 129
Turkish eggs 84
Turkish sour 218
Tuscan chickpea and vegetable soup 67

Vegetables
Tuscan chickpea and vegetable soup 67

Watermelon
feta, watermelon and pitta crisp
  salad 136
Welsh rarebit and leek sandwiches 80
Whiting
Warm Indian quinoa salad with whiting,
  grapes and almonds 108
Wraps, Lebanese lamb 137

Acknowledgements

I properly started work on this book a few months before I gave birth to Twiglet, our second child. It was a mad undertaking and almost killed me but I loved (almost) every bit of its creation. A handful of amazing, kind people helped me along the way. Without them I would simply not have been able to do it.

Thank you to Rebe for being the most amazing addition to our household. Without her continuous support, humour, teasing and fun I am not sure any of us would survive. She is the best.

Thank you to everyone at Hodder for making this as smooth a ride as it could have been with a brand new baby to look after. To Alasdair Oliver, Kate Brunt, Susan Spratt, the wonderful Emma Knight and in particular Nicky Ross and Sarah Hammond for never questioning my delays or seeming to doubt my ability to finish this book. And Zelda Turner, for editing yet another of my books with good sense and razor sharp mind.

Thank you to the creative team for spending two weeks at home with me cooking and shooting the book: Emma Miller, for endless patience, brilliant testing, incredibly organised prowess, great gossip and wonderful nature; Tabitha Hawkins for finally working with me and doing such a brilliant job; those über-talented boys at Burocreative, in particular Roly and Jo-Jo, the love of Tati's life; Tara Fisher for coming back and shooting with such passion – I didn't believe we would have as good a time as last time but we did!

To my mates: all of you who tasted some chilli notes, inspired them or were just around whilst I was in the midst of the chaos, thank you for being you – I love you all.

To all my testers: Jules, Dee, Cecilia and of course Emma, thank you, thank you – and to Carolyn Chan, Lin and Flo for excellent Malay knowledge.

To Mark, my brilliant business partner, Rosie, my endlessly patient and helpful PA and the team at Wahaca for being there, keeping me young and giving me so much.

To Anna Barrett, my gap year travelling buddy who lured me to Mexico in the first place (what a riot!).

Most of all to my saint-like parents who upended their lives to house me and two small girls for a month, who endlessly tested and copy-edited, who gave me notes and judicious improvements on recipes, who are never afraid to tell me when something isn't good enough. You guys rock. Seriously. I am very very lucky.

Lastly to Mark Williams who had to cope with my sheer exhaustion whilst I wrote this. I hope it wasn't too hellish, especially eating all those chillies. Thank you for endless sage advice, support, love and a few wild nights along the way.